ART BY JOHNNY

a collection of work from
Johnny Carroll-Pell

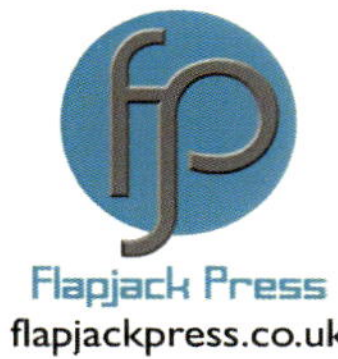

Flapjack Press
flapjackpress.co.uk

Published in 2018 by Flapjack Press
Salford, Gtr Manchester
flapjackpress.co.uk

ISBN 978-0-9955012-9-4

Facebook: Art By Johnny

Printed by Imprint Digital
Upton Pyne, Exeter, Devon
imprintdigital.com

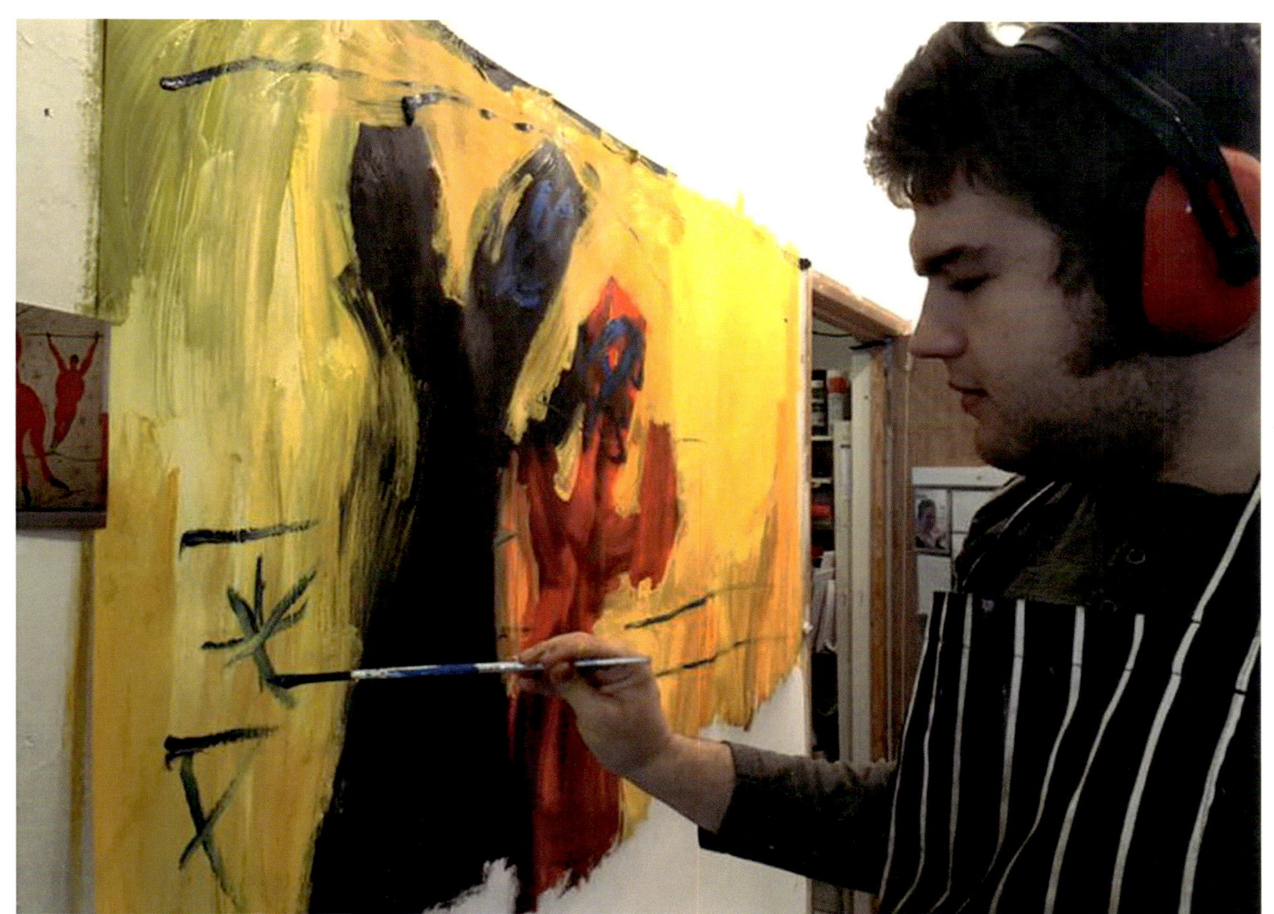

Two Circus Figures
Johnny painting at
his first session with
The Rocket Artists.
Inspired by Maxwell
Holyoke-Hirsch
painting.
Acrylic on paper,
2016.

JOHNNY'S USE OF COLOUR and mark-making are purely intuitive. His mastery of colour and tone both attract the viewer's gaze and then, in what is perhaps the most difficult action of an artist, holds it. The mark-making is energetic and immerses you into Johnny's world of intense sensual experience; colours, lights, movement and feelings are magnified and an incredible door is held slightly ajar for the viewer to generously share Johnny's vision.

Memory, repetition, nostalgia and ritual appear important in the communication Johnny conveys. It is instinctive and quick, and somehow reflects the world in which we live in today: the vast speed of information and data, the flow of energetic impulses and quickfire decisions, the routines which we all live by but take for granted, the strange nature of traditional iconic buildings or cartoons or seaside character performances (seaside pavilions, Kung Fu Panda, etc) which spark a feeling of nostalgia for us all. Johnny receives this information and slows it down for the viewer to be able to receive and digest.

Watching Johnny create is performative in its nature of watching someone make something a reality, and for me so incredibly inspiring. Johnny's self-editing ability is fast. He is quickly aware and certain of what he wants to action and what marks to make. The ego is not a voice that comes to play loudly within this process. *"Will people like it?" "Is this right?" "Is this the right tone?"* – these decisions are intuitive and natural for Johnny, and incredibly fast. His priority appears to be the process, and as he creates it is as if he is creating a moving image or film. To have that level of certainty as an artist is rare. The historic story of an artist in turmoil over whether a creation is 'worthy' is not something that is of interest to Johnny. His need as a visual communicator is to convey his world as he sees it, no filter, no edits. In a world where we are viewers to so many snapshots of others' daily experiences through social media and heavily filtered and edited platforms, Johnny's raw expression and platform is fresh, powerful, energetic and incredibly insightful.

Johnny is an incredibly accomplished artist and he has hit the zeitgeist of what it is to experience life today in the UK.

Laura Keeble
British artist

I LEARN LOTS WHEN WORKING with Johnny and he's helped me think more about the physical act of painting in terms of time and scale. I'm aware that when we work together some extremes are at play; large and small, loud and quiet, fast and slow... and that time appears to stretch and contract like elastic.

There are the wonderful expanded minutes when we navigate the space around each other to find the best angle to cut a piece of stretchy fabric into strips for his weaving. Or as we slowly unreel the silky tape from a discarded Blow Monkeys VHS.

Then there are the very still moments when we are waiting, tensed around the stretcher, listening for the feeling of the moment the staple punches out through the canvas and into the wooden frame. Ready bang.

And then there are the moments that I step back – Johnny armed with paint and brushes and ideas, owning the space around him. I glance up and around the rest of the studio, momentarily. And in those seconds, he's created something so fresh and so exuberant, so engaging and *SO* fast!

Jo Offer
Rocket Artists

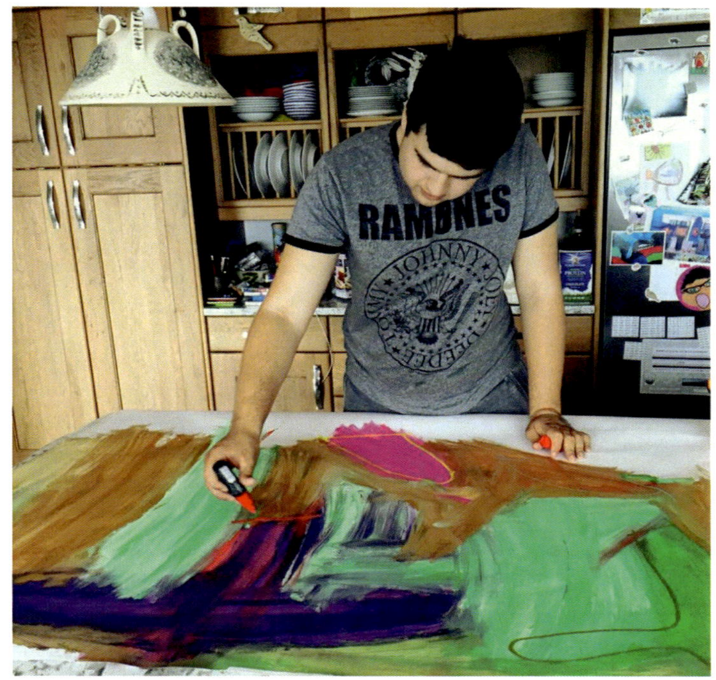

Johnny Posca-ing *Hills and Trees* in the kitchen, 2017.

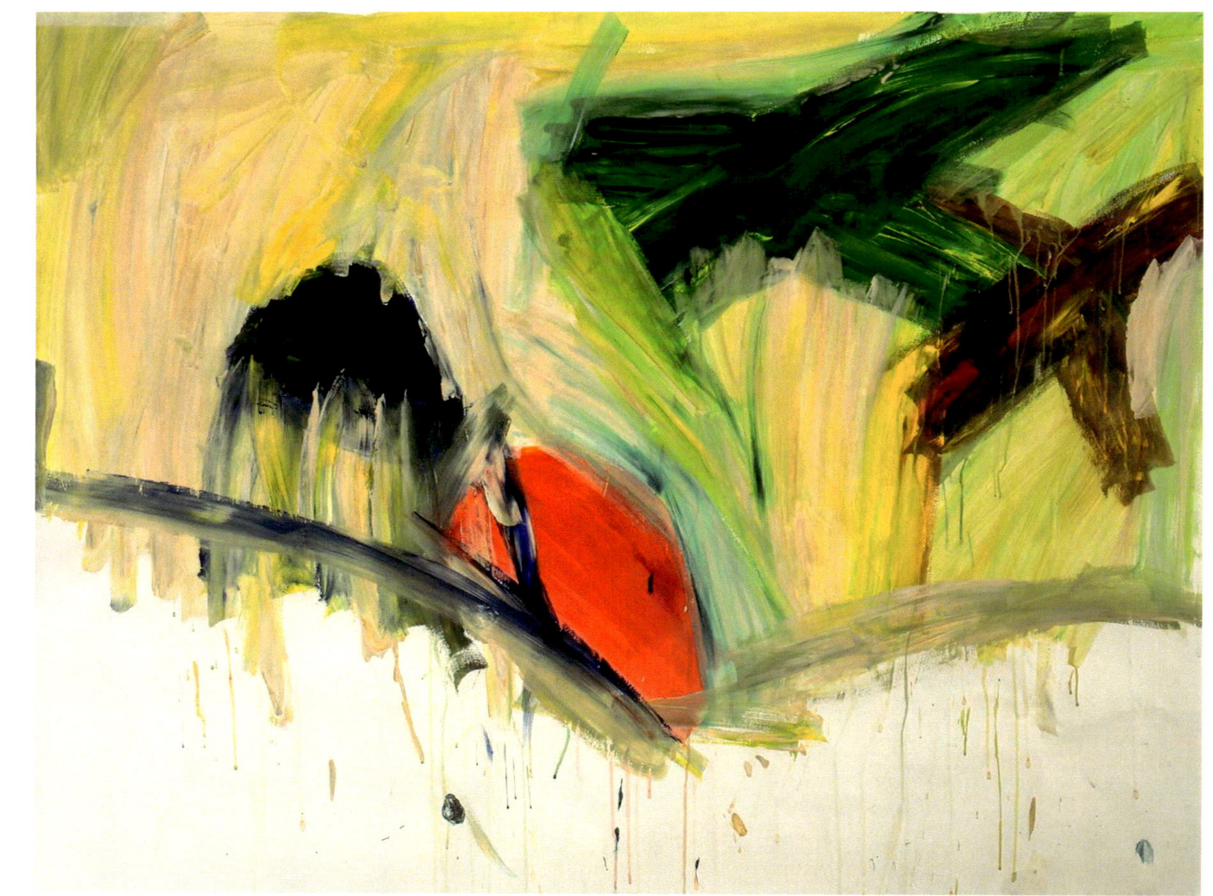

Hills and Trees
A Saturday afternoon painting. A detail of this painting was used on the cover of Johnny's dad's 2017 poetry book *Raining Upwards*. Acrylic on paper.

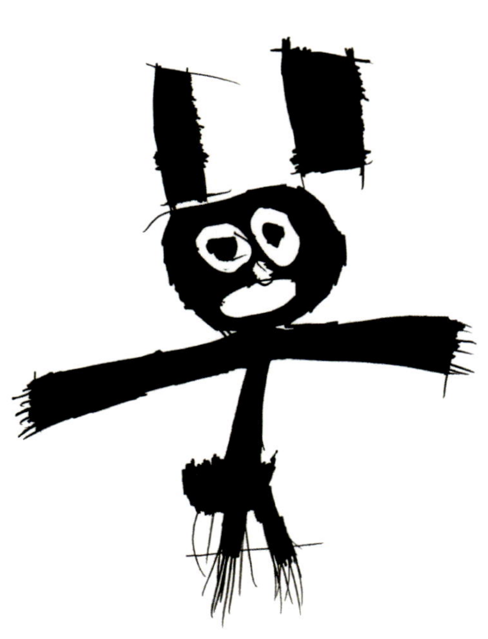

Early *Kung Fu Panda* figure.
Black permanent marker pen
on canvas, c.2012, 44cm x 60cm.

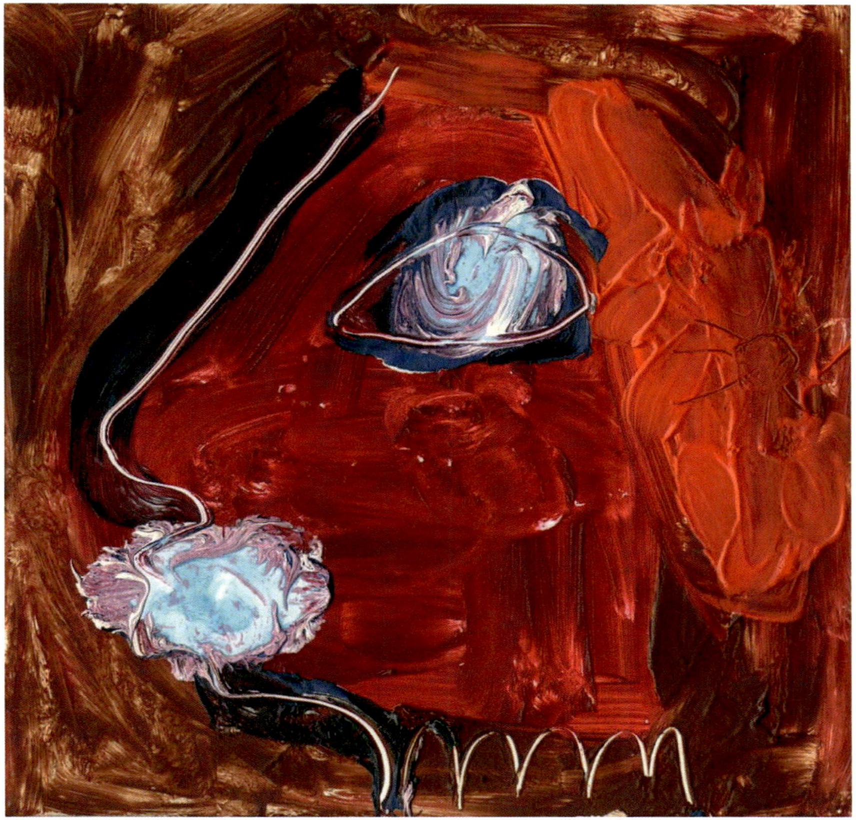

Deep Red Face
Oil paint on a kitchen tile, c.2014, 20cm x 20cm.

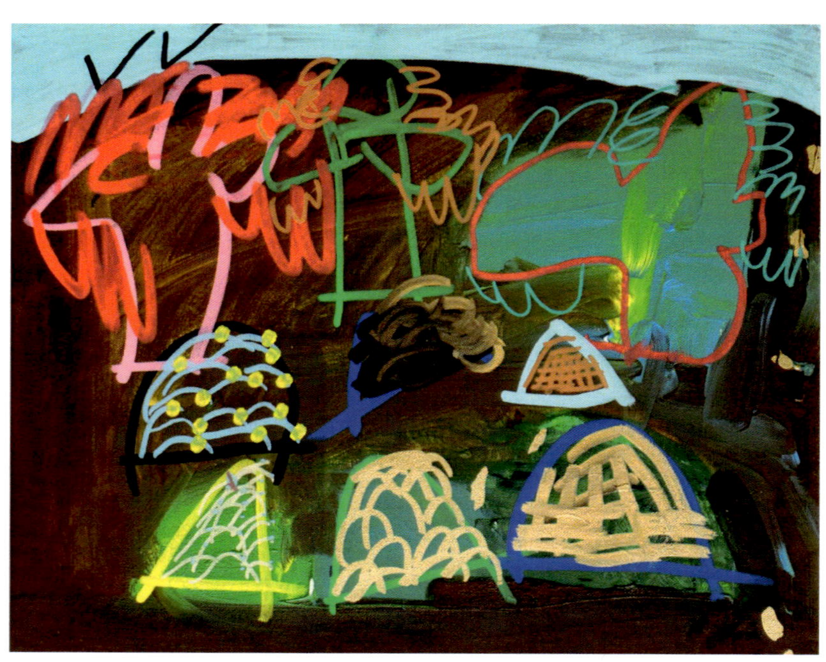

Fields and Crops
Old canvas board painting with new Posca pen detail,
2017, 50cm x 40cm.

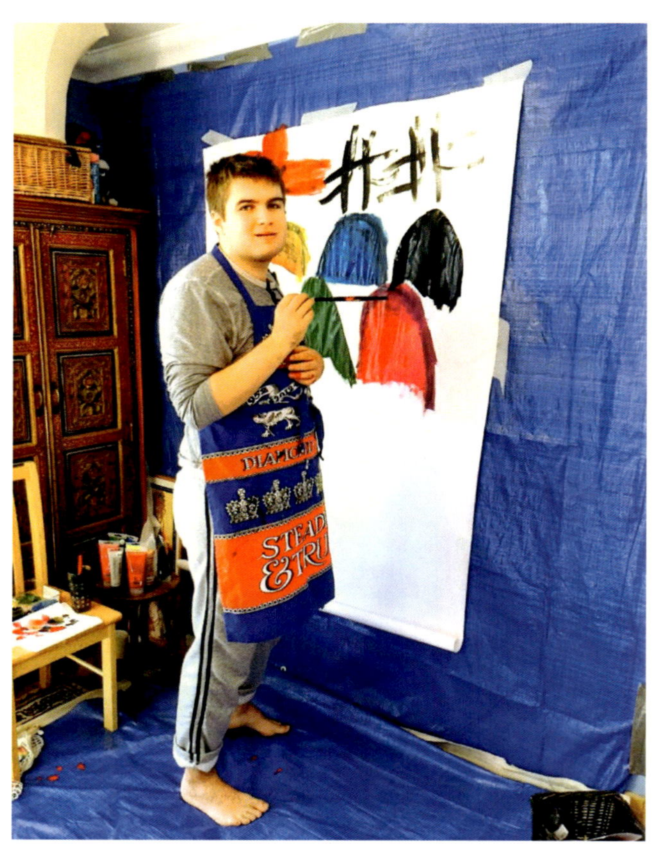

Johnny barefoot, painting *Hills and Trees*.
Acrylic on paper, 2014.

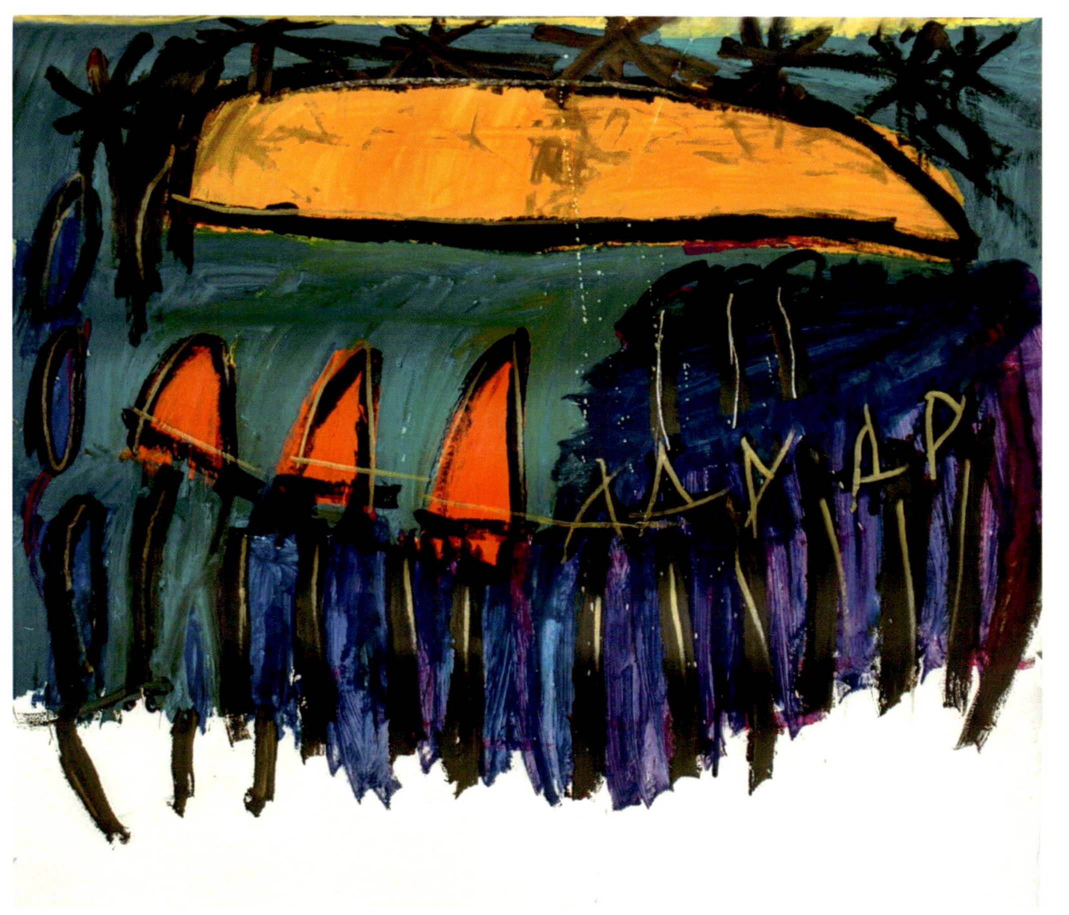

Mountains
Painted at Rocket
Artists Studio.
Inspired by Maxwell
Holyoke-Hirsch drawing.
Acrylic on paper.

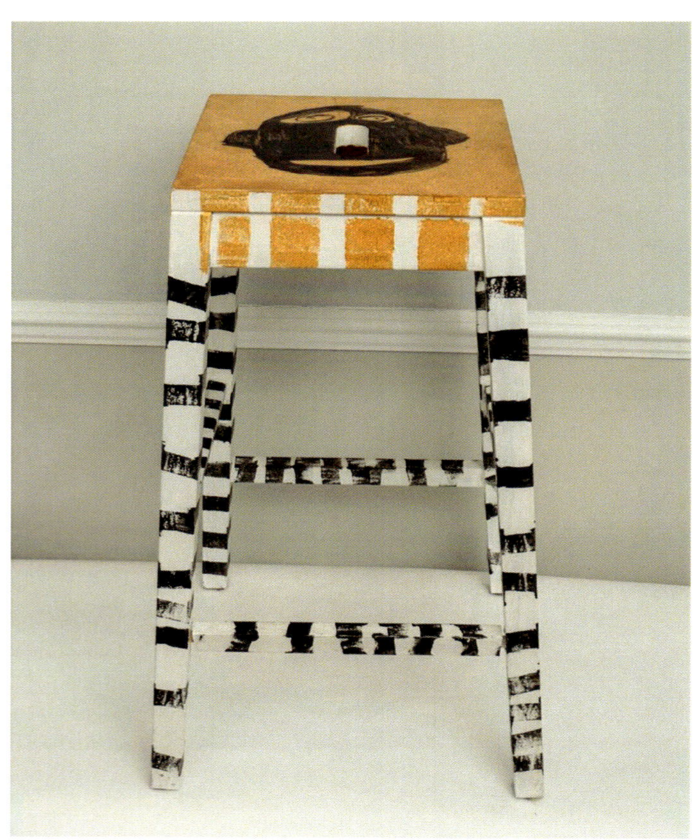

Kitchen Stool
One of three, 2014.

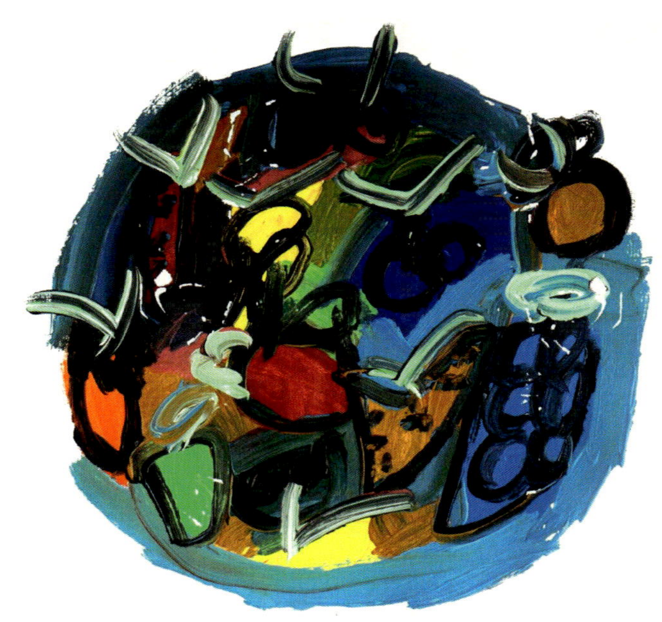

Fruit Bowl
Inspired by a painted plate.
Acrylic on canvas paper, 2016.

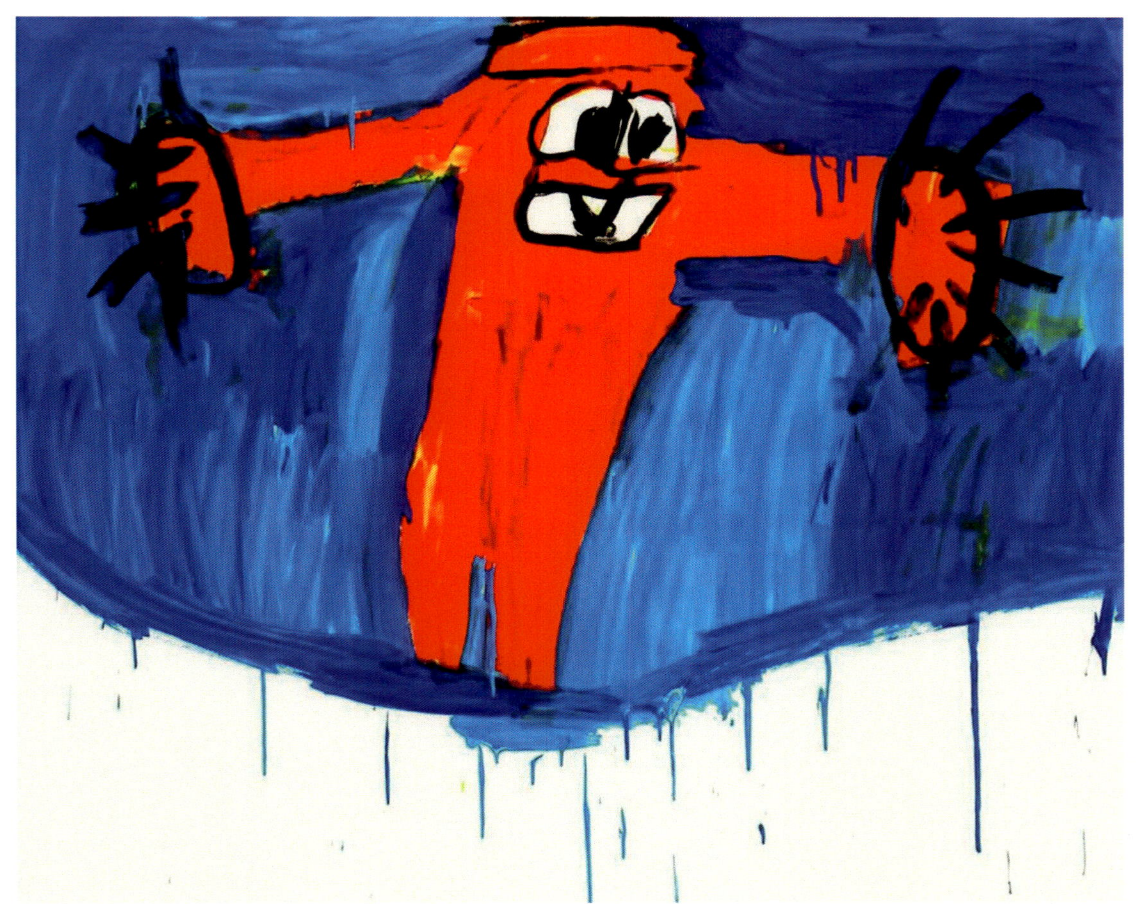

Nick Cave
Copy of a photograph
on the iPad.
This painting was later
selected to go into a
'coffee table book' of
pictures by fans, which
was handed to Nick Cave
for his 60th birthday.
Acrylic on paper, 2017,
151cm x 130cm.

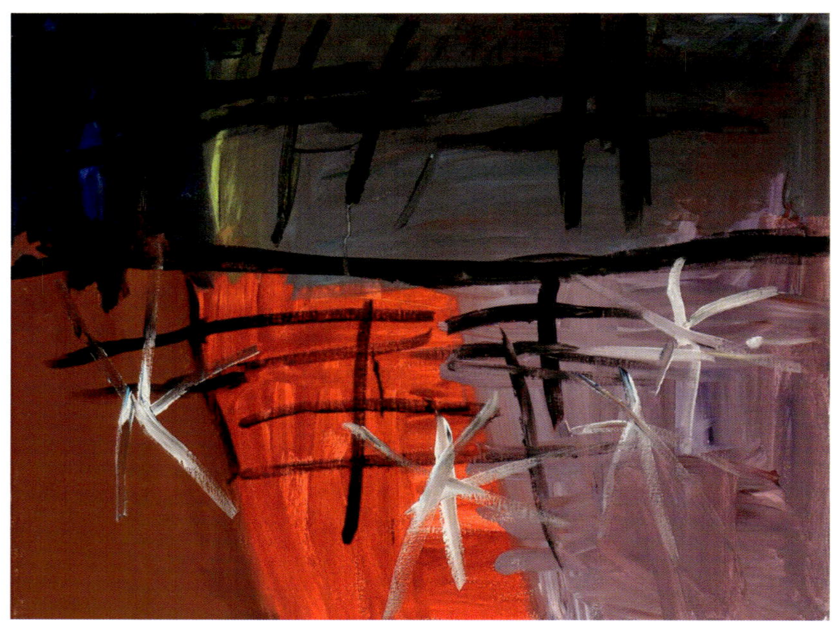

Water Lilies on the Lake
Painted at Sacred Earth Land Project, Horam,
during Johnny's Friday 'Farm Buddies' sessions there.
Acrylic on canvas, 2017, 76cm x 60cm.

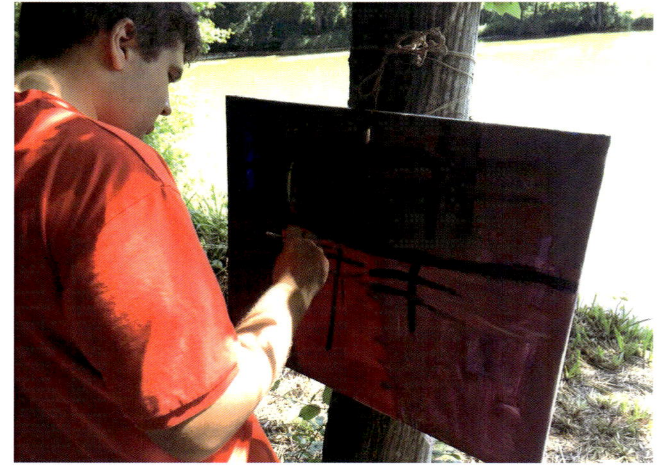

Johnny painting the lake at
Sacred Earth Land Project.

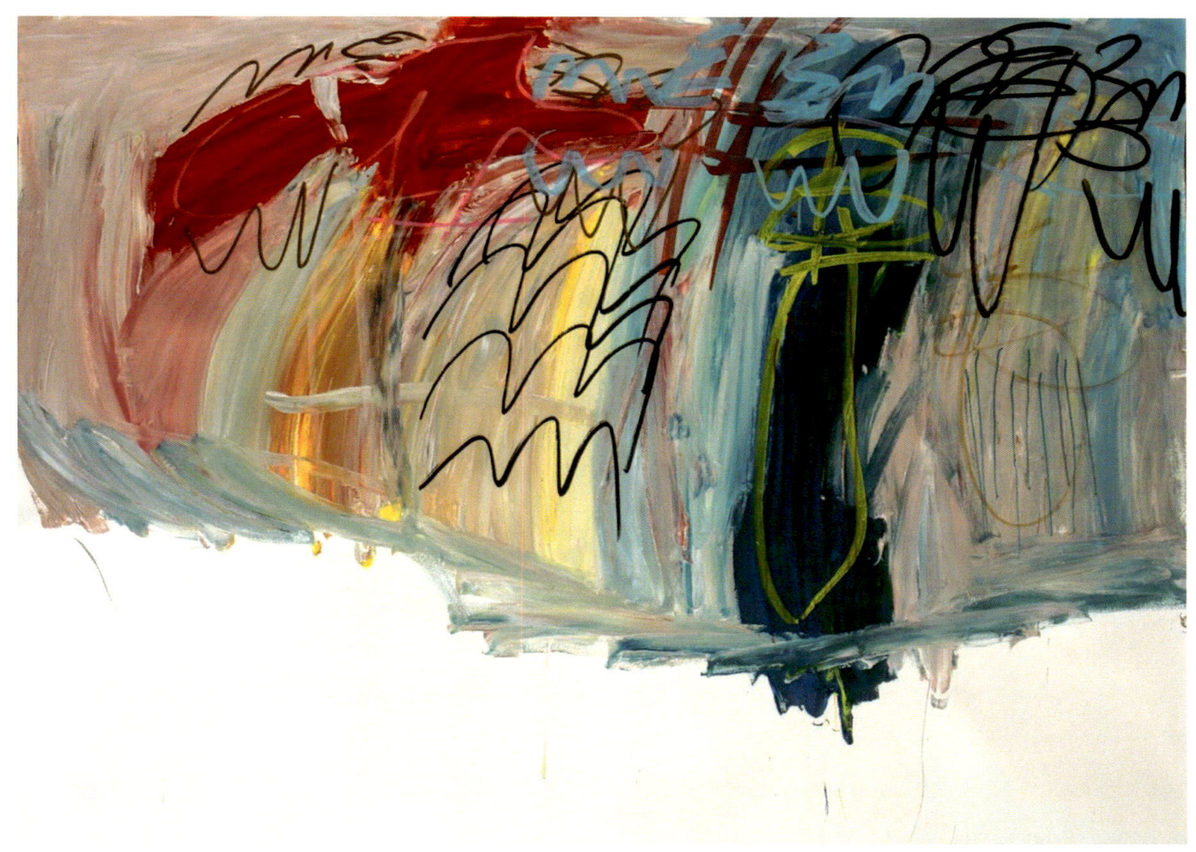

Villa, Pool, Parasol and Pot Plant
Acrylic on paper with Posca pen, 2017, 151cm x 104cm.

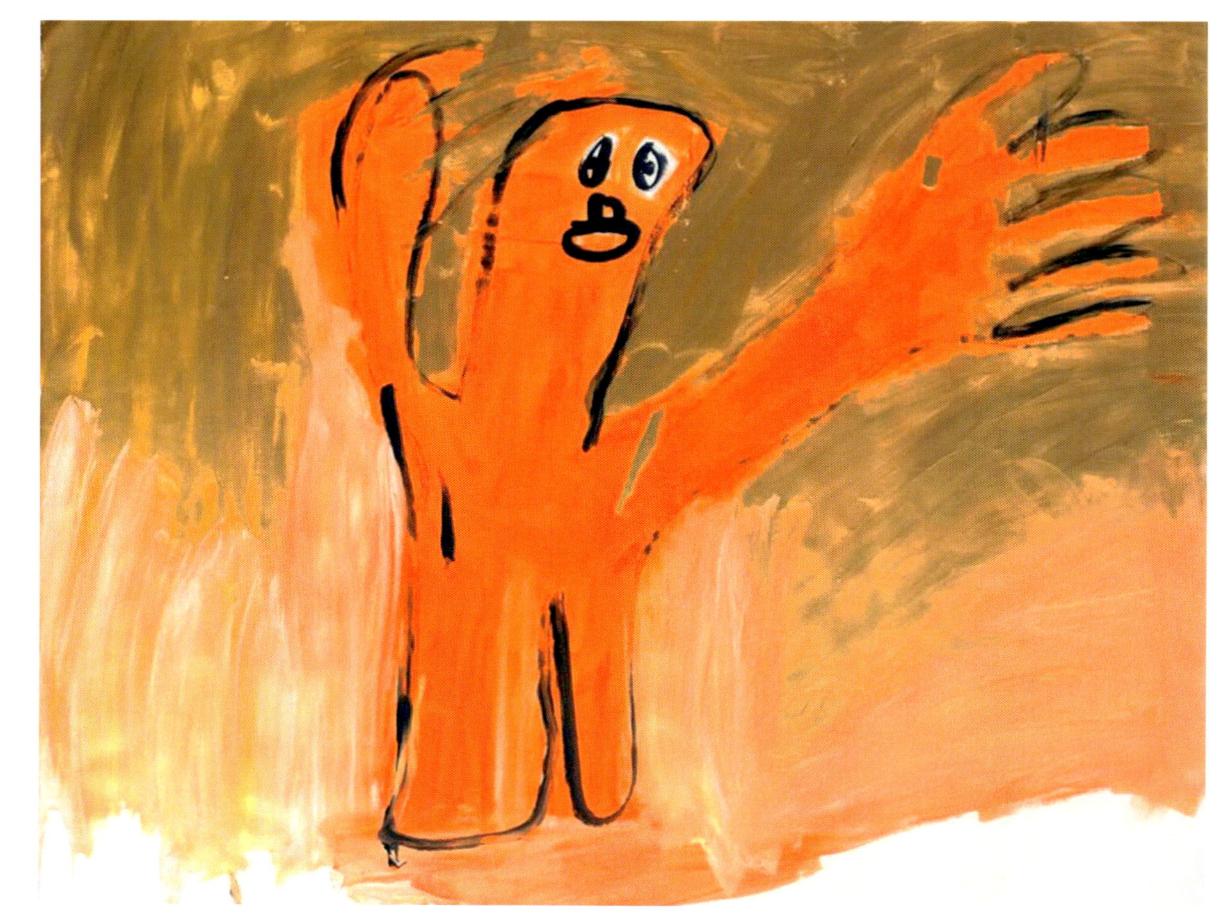

Orange Man
Acrylic on paper,
2017, 151cm x
138cm.

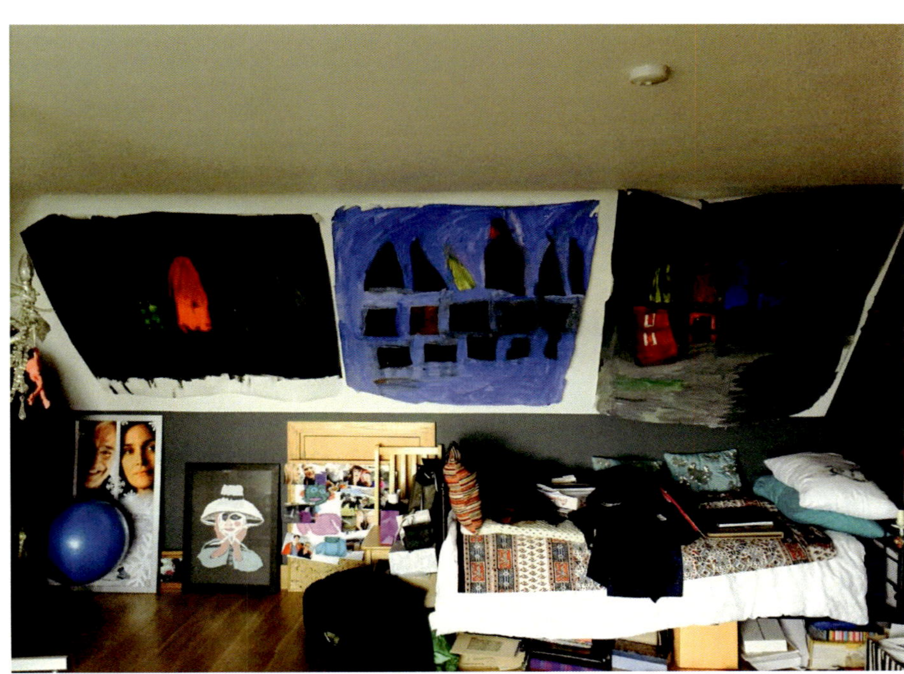

Three *Pavilion* paintings hung in Johnny's mum's office.
Acrylic on paper, c.2014.

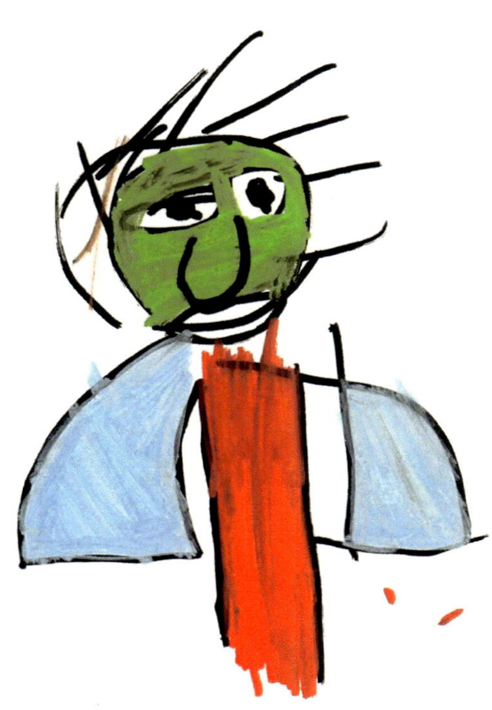

Portrait of Johnny's mother.
Felt pen on paper, 2016, 14cm x 20cm.

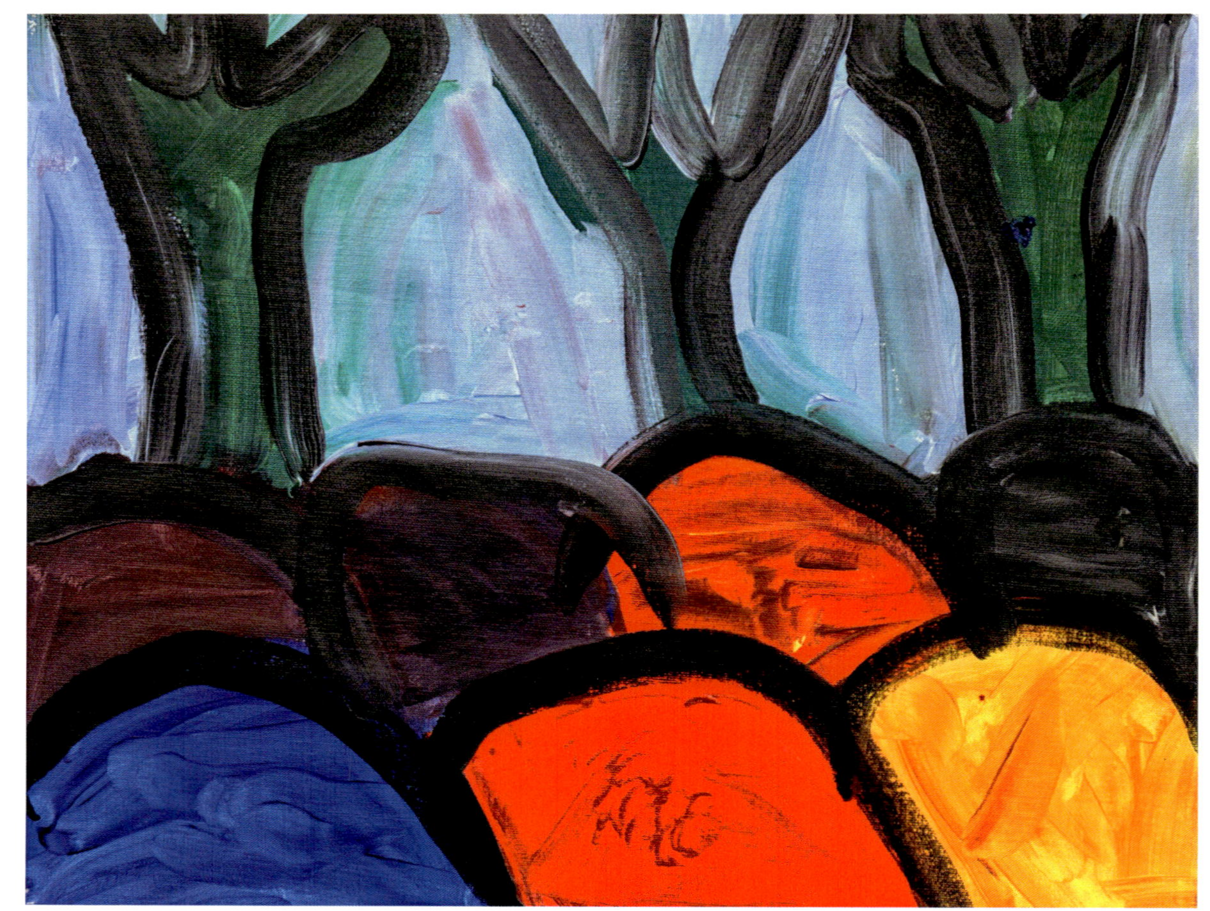

Early
Hills and Trees.
Acrylic on
canvas board,
c.2013,
50cm x 40cm.

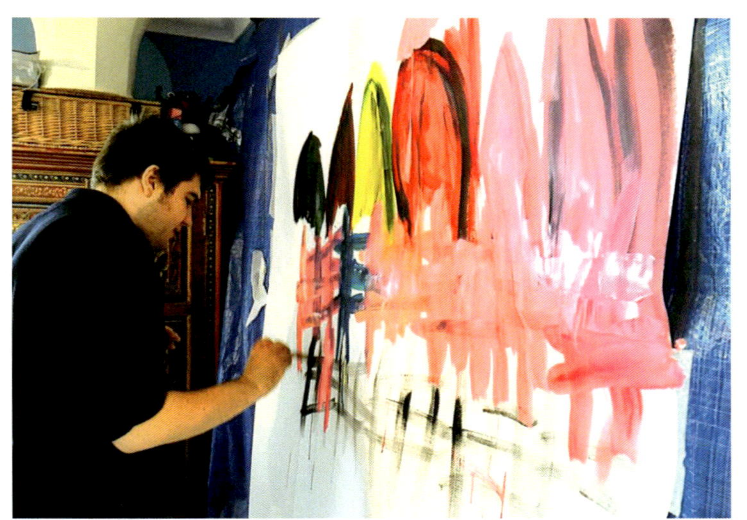

Johnny painting Brighton Pavilion.
Acrylic on paper, 2015.

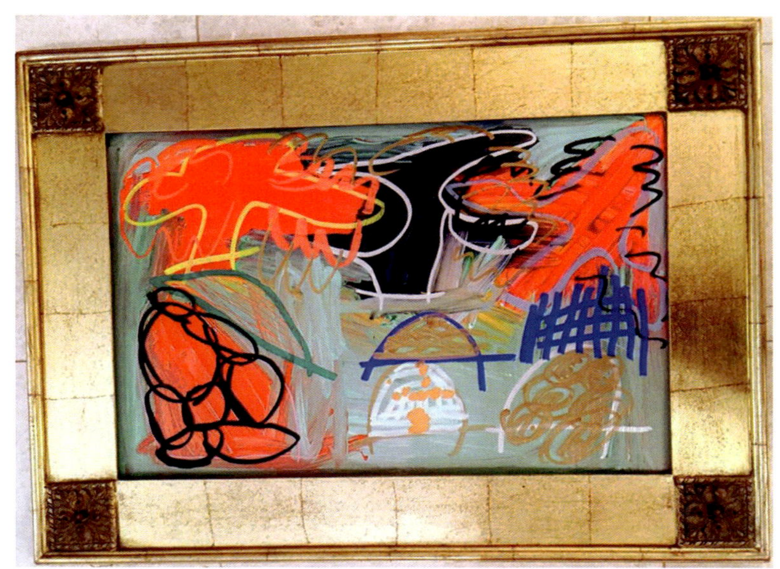

Hills, Trees and Crops
Acrylic with added Posca pen on backing board of frame,
76cm x 52cm.
Photographed with gold frame, 2018.

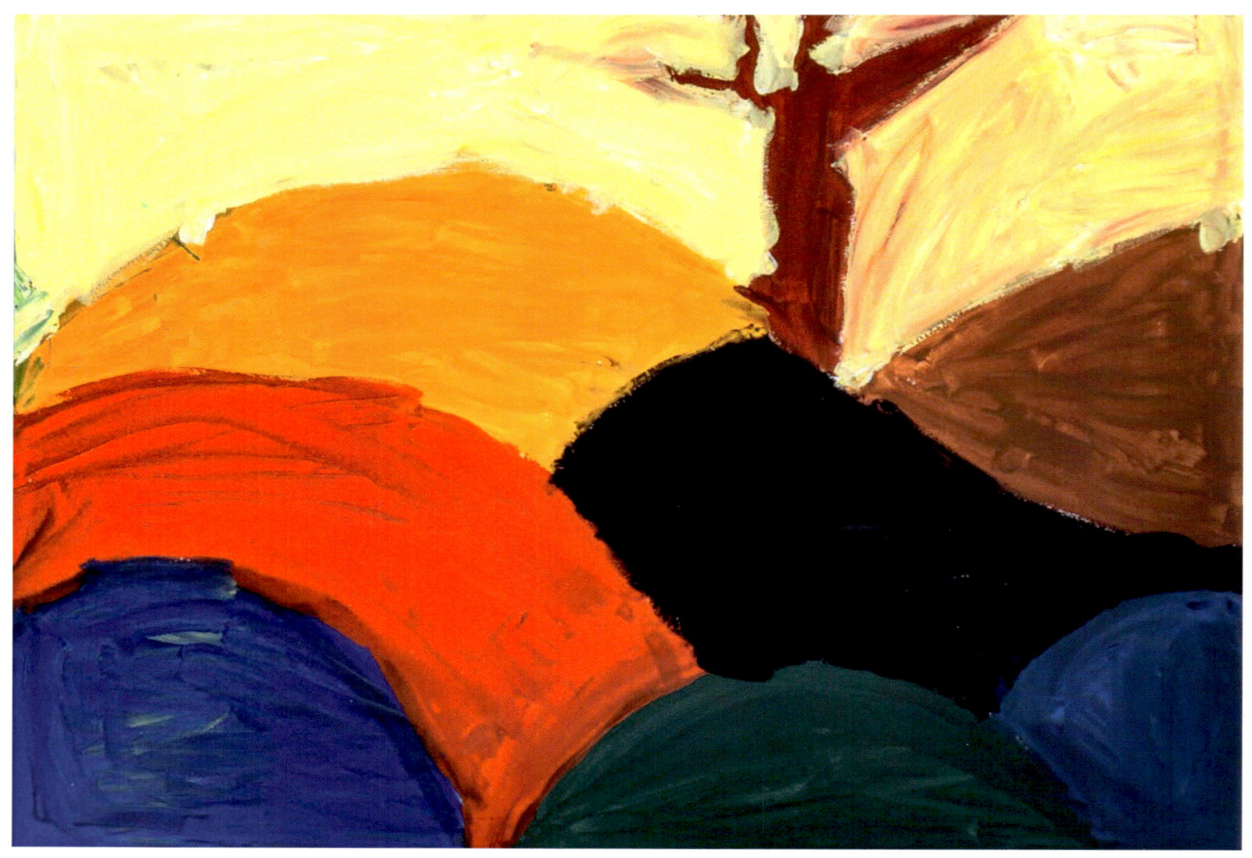

Hills and Trees
Acrylic on paper, c.2013, 60cm x 42cm.

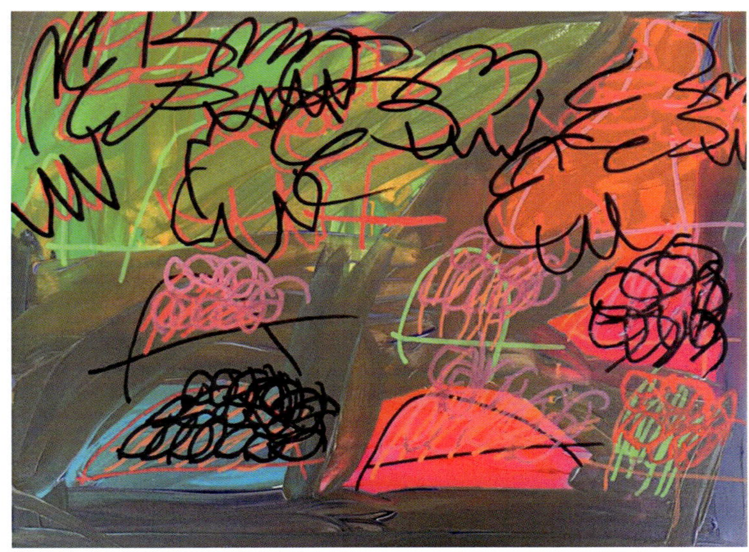

Hills and Trees Revisited
Very old canvas board painting painted in Portugal, c.2012.
With newly added Posca pen, 2017, 41cm x 29cm.

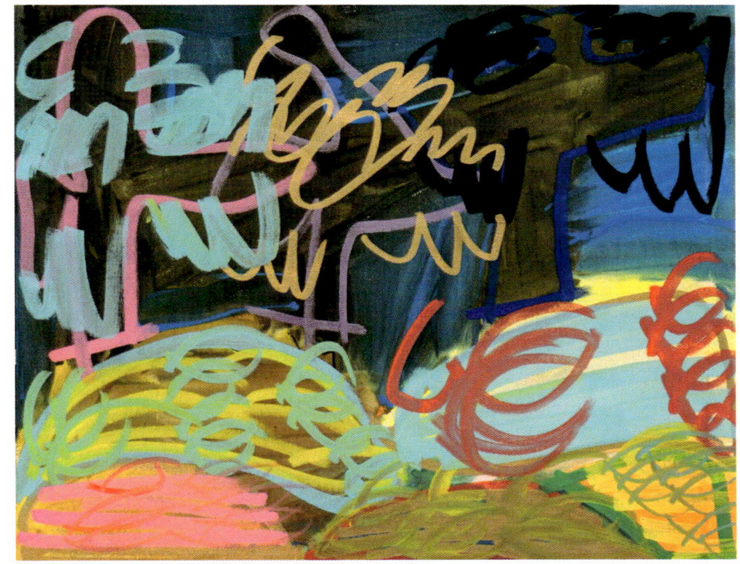

Hills and Trees
Acrylic on canvas with added Posca pen, 50cm x 40cm.

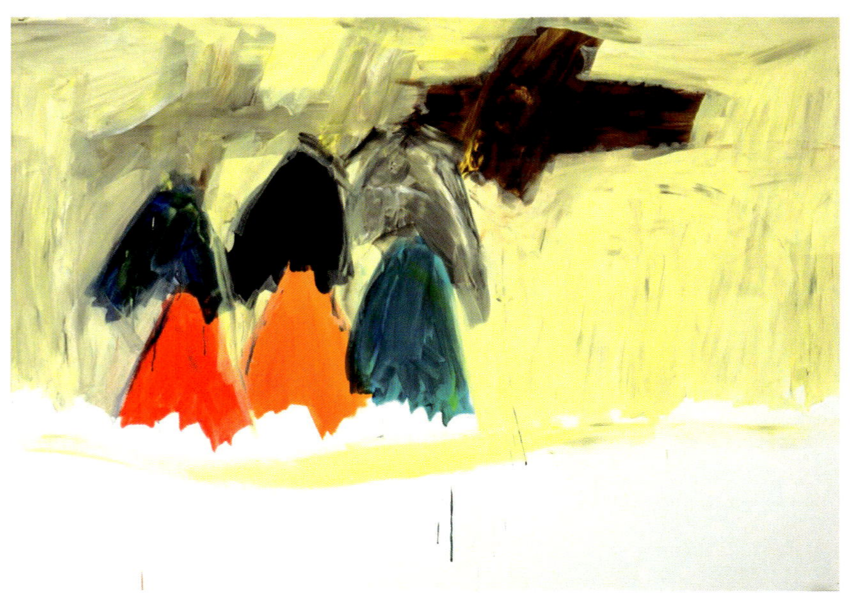

Early *Hills and Trees*.
Acrylic on paper,
c.2014, 151cm x 87cm.

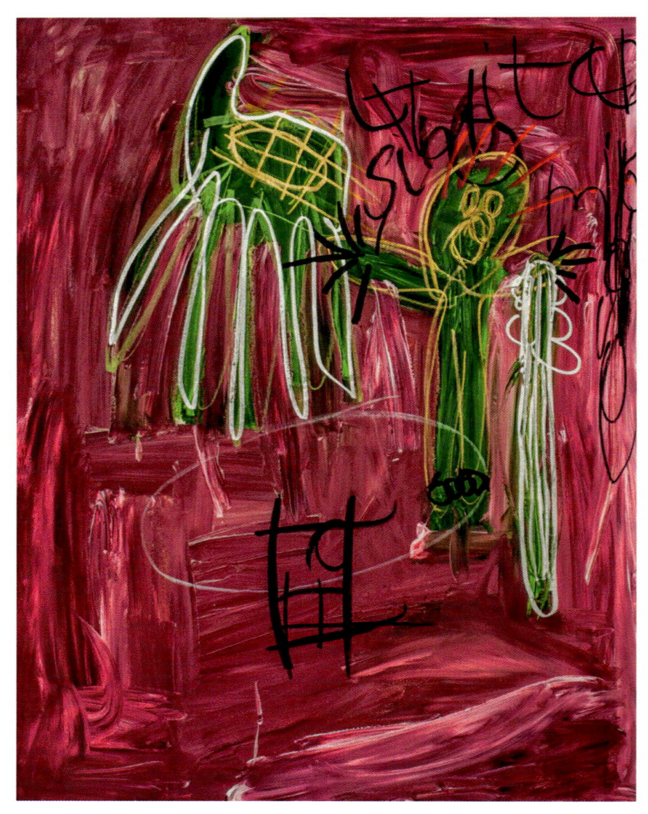

Tom and Guitar
Acrylic on canvas with writing,
2017, 94cm x 122cm.

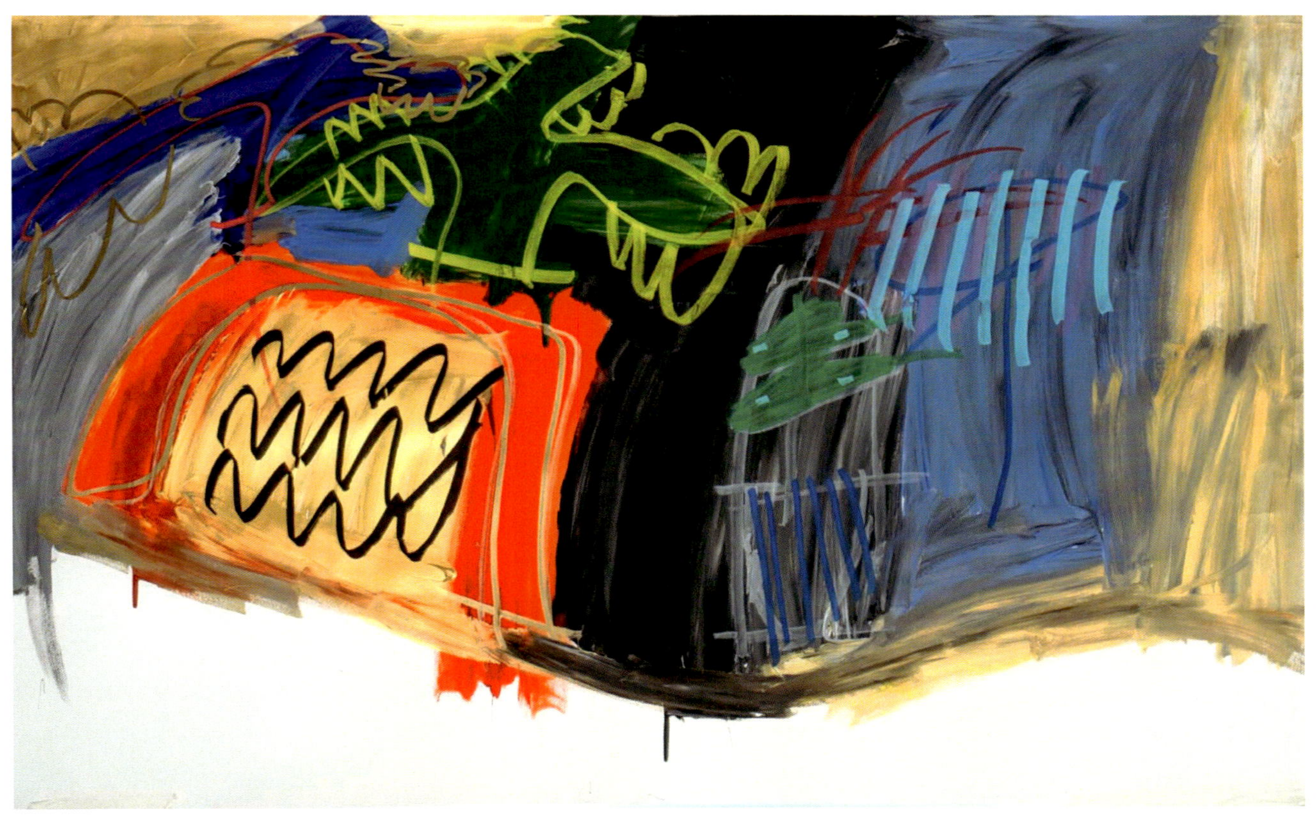

Villa and Pool
Acrylic on paper with added Posca pen,
2017, 151cm x 86cm.

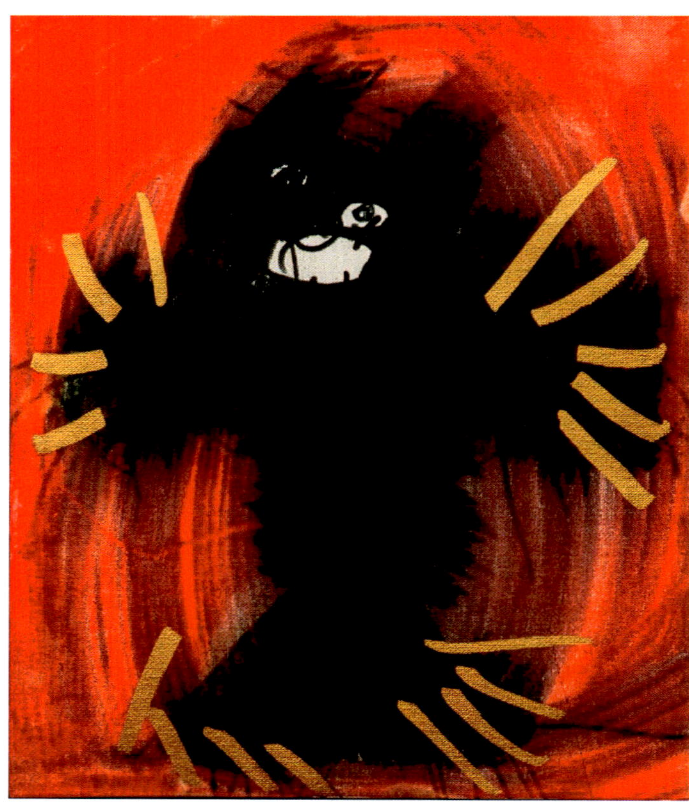

Kung Fu Panda
Permanent marker, felt tip and gold paint pen
on canvas board, 2017, 25cm x 30cm.

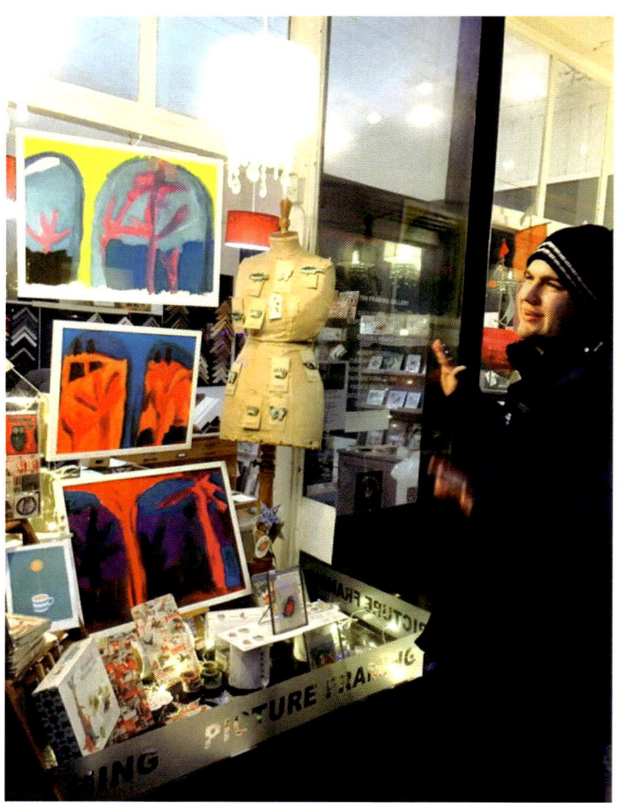

Johnny seeing his paintings
on display in the window of
The Brighton Framing Gallery, 2015.

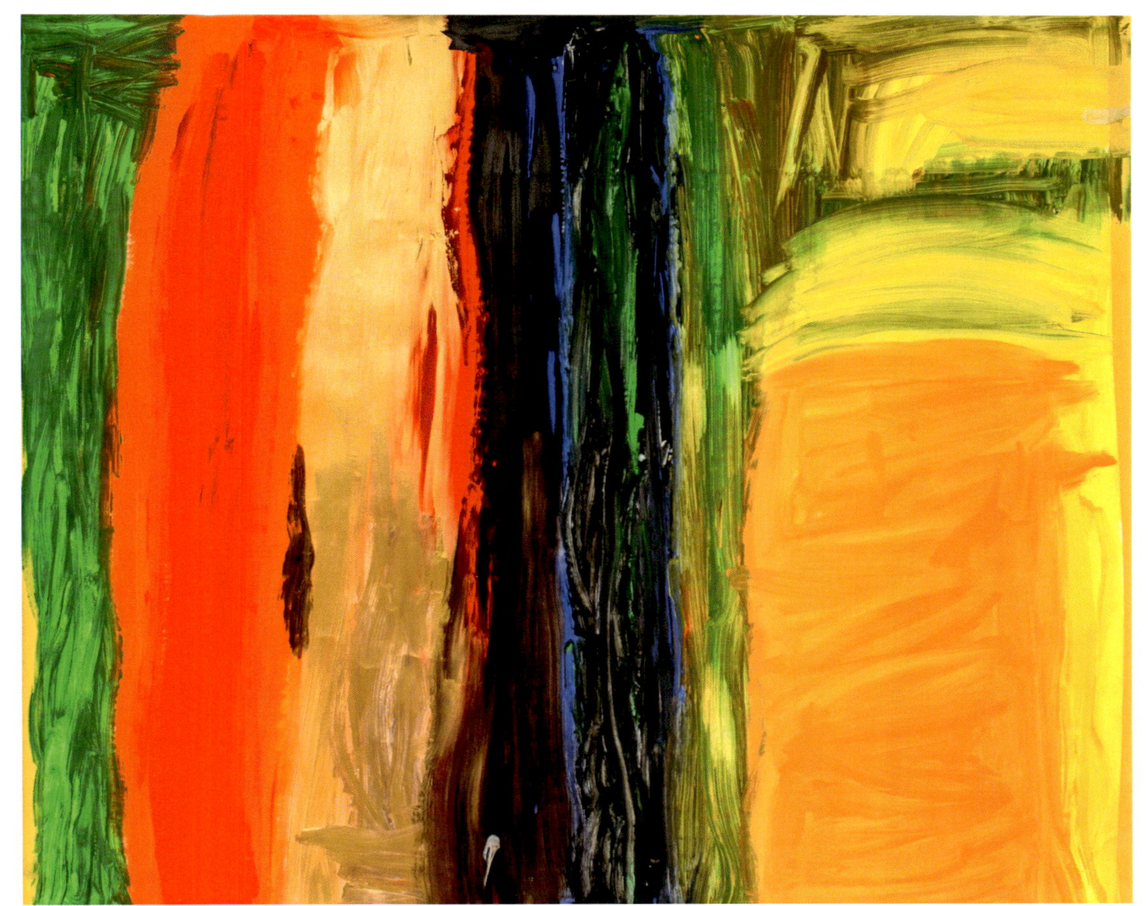

Colours
Painted at Project
Artworks Hastings.
Acrylic on canvas,
February 2016,
183cm x 151cm.

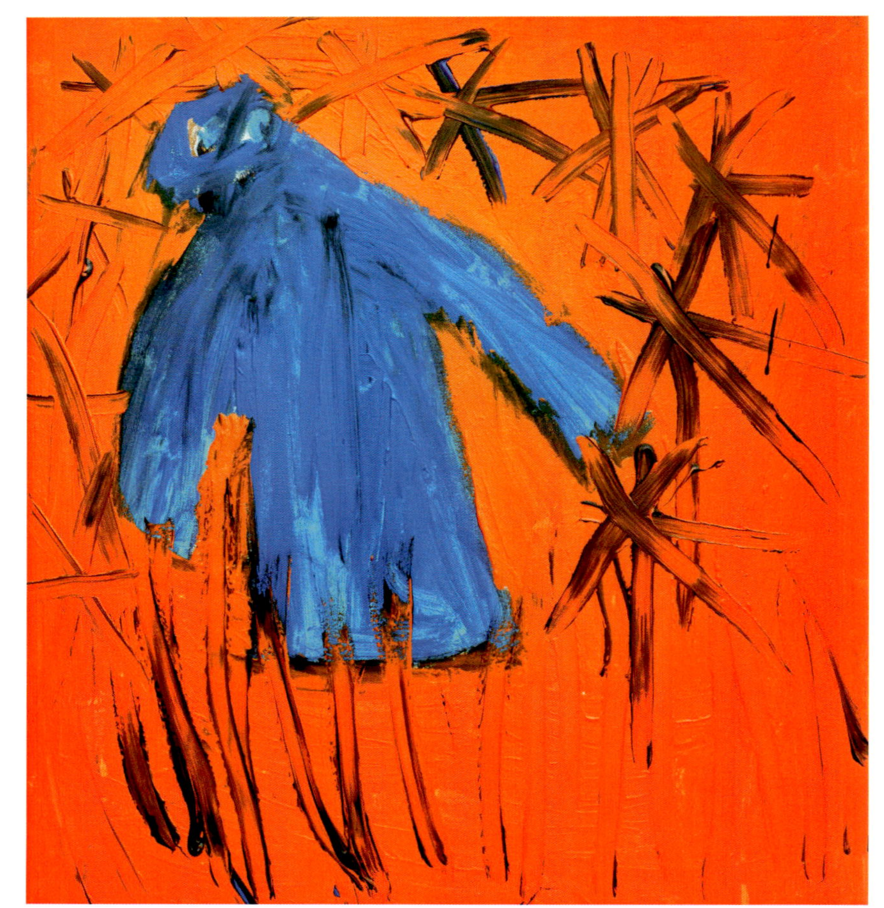

Blue Man on Orange Background
Painted at Rocket Artists Studio.
Inspired by Maxwell
Holyoke-Hirsch painting.
Acrylic on canvas, 2017,
80cm x 100cm.

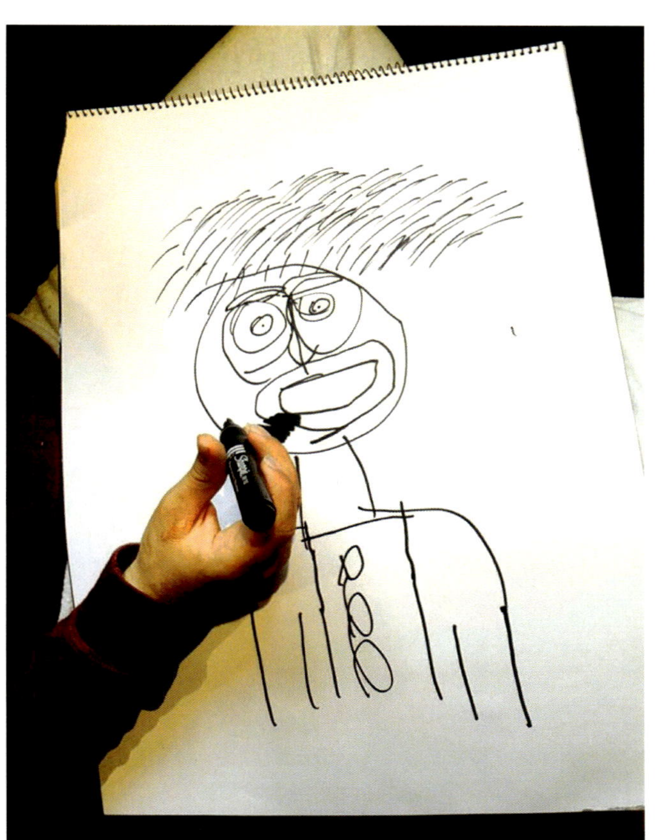

Johnny drawing a self-portrait, 2016.

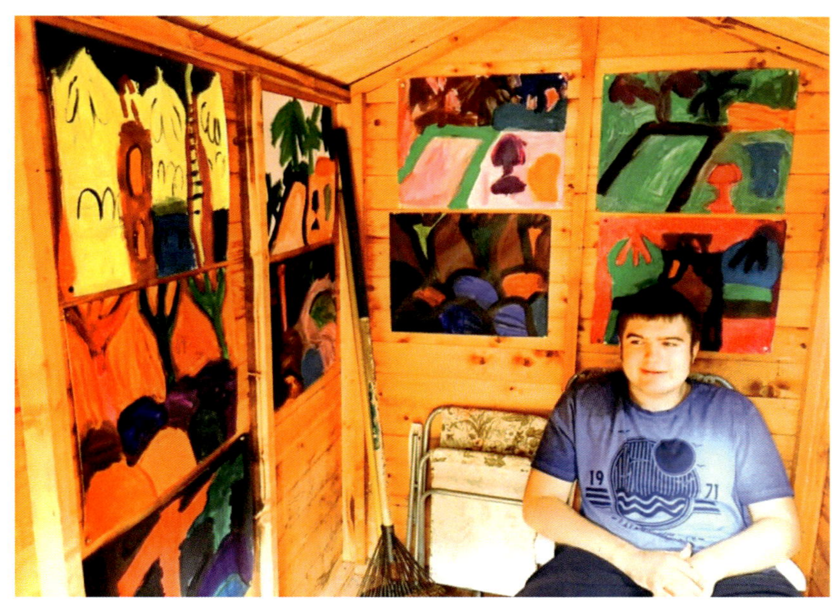

Johnny with his paintings in his makeshift
garden shed gallery, 2014.

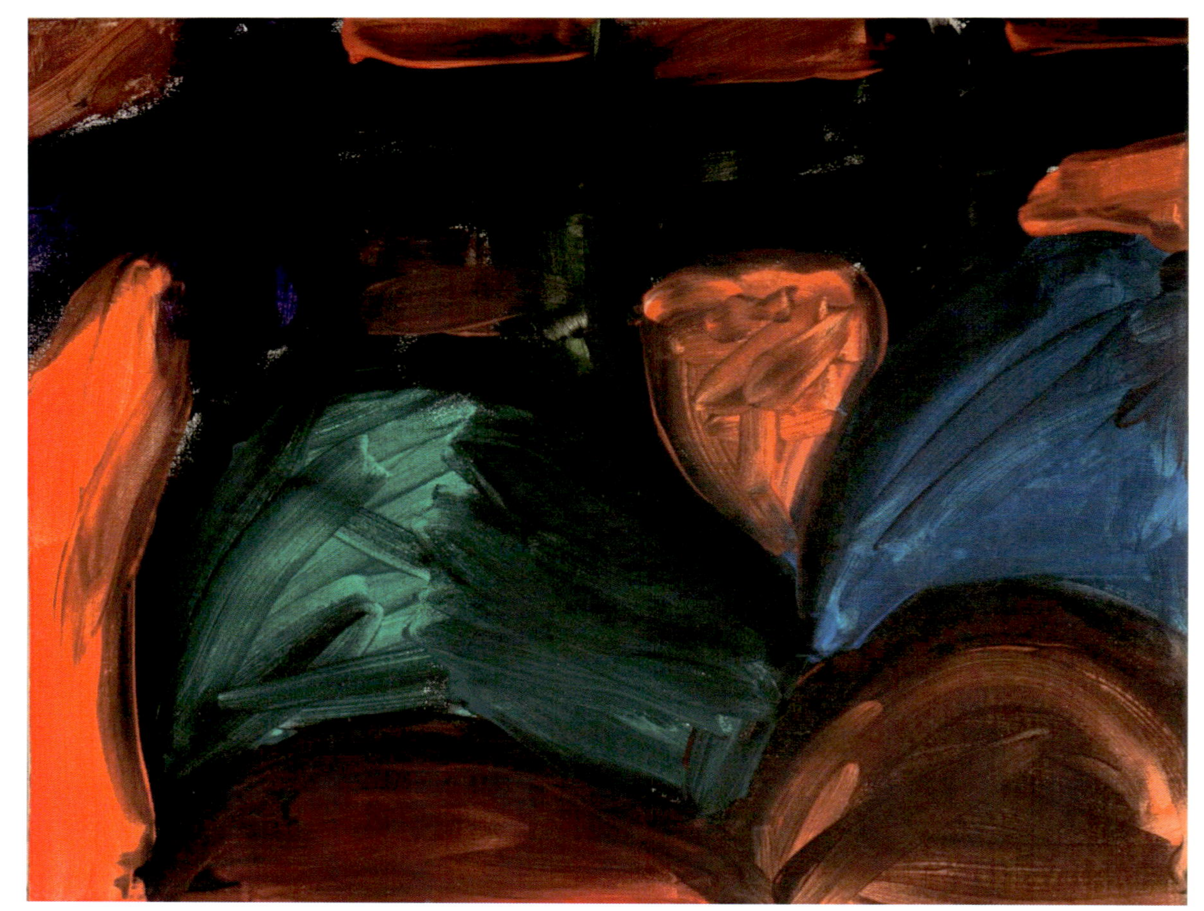

Early *Hills and Trees* painting. Acrylic on canvas board, 2014.

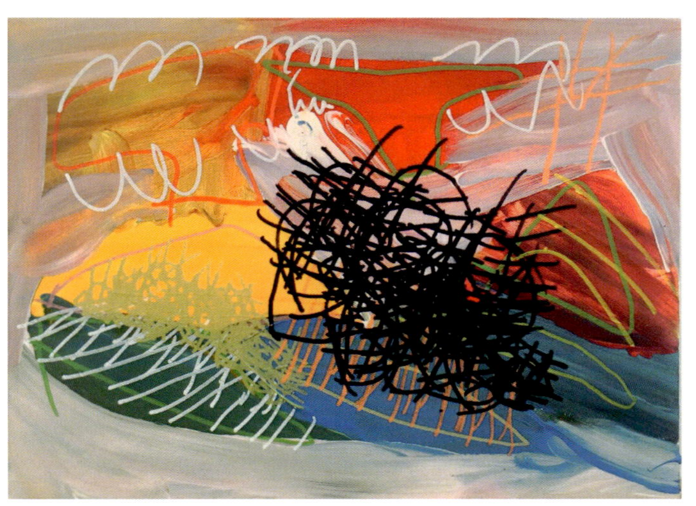

Hills, Trees and Crops
Painted in Portugal.
Acrylic on canvas board, 2017.

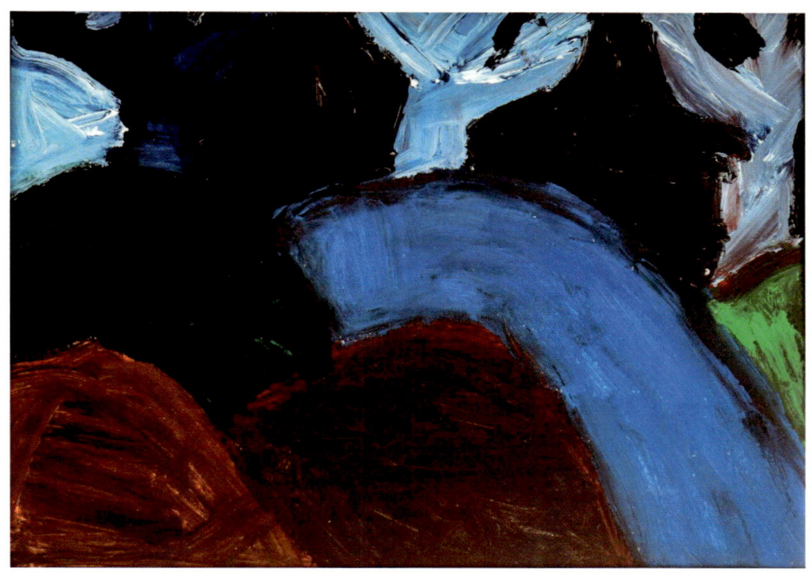

Hills and Trees
Acrylic on cardboard, c.2012, 40cm x 30cm.

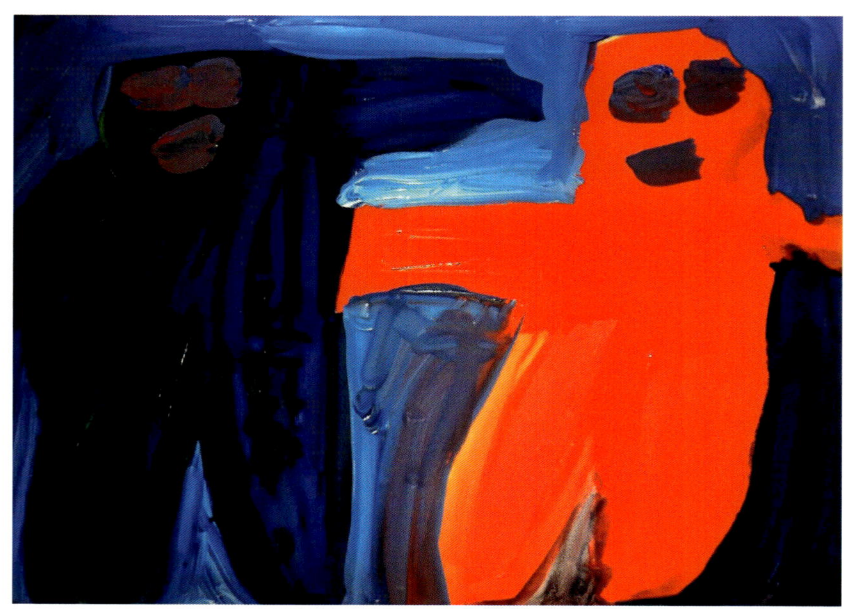

Red and Blue Man
This painting was used as the cover for Johnny's dad's poetry book
Staring Directly at the Eclipse, published in 2016.
Acrylic on cardboard, 65cm x 50cm.

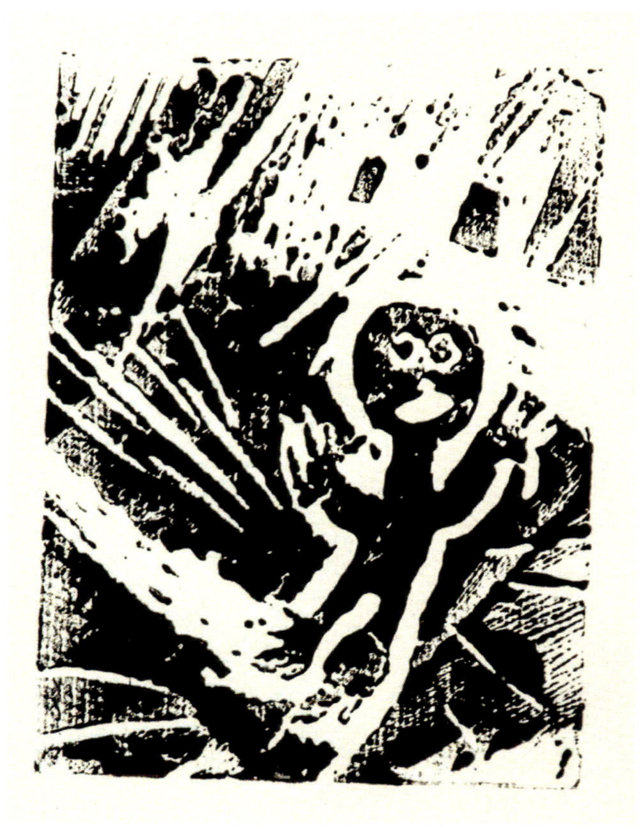

Kung Fu Panda
First attempt at lino printing.
Ink on paper, 2016, 14cm x 17cm.

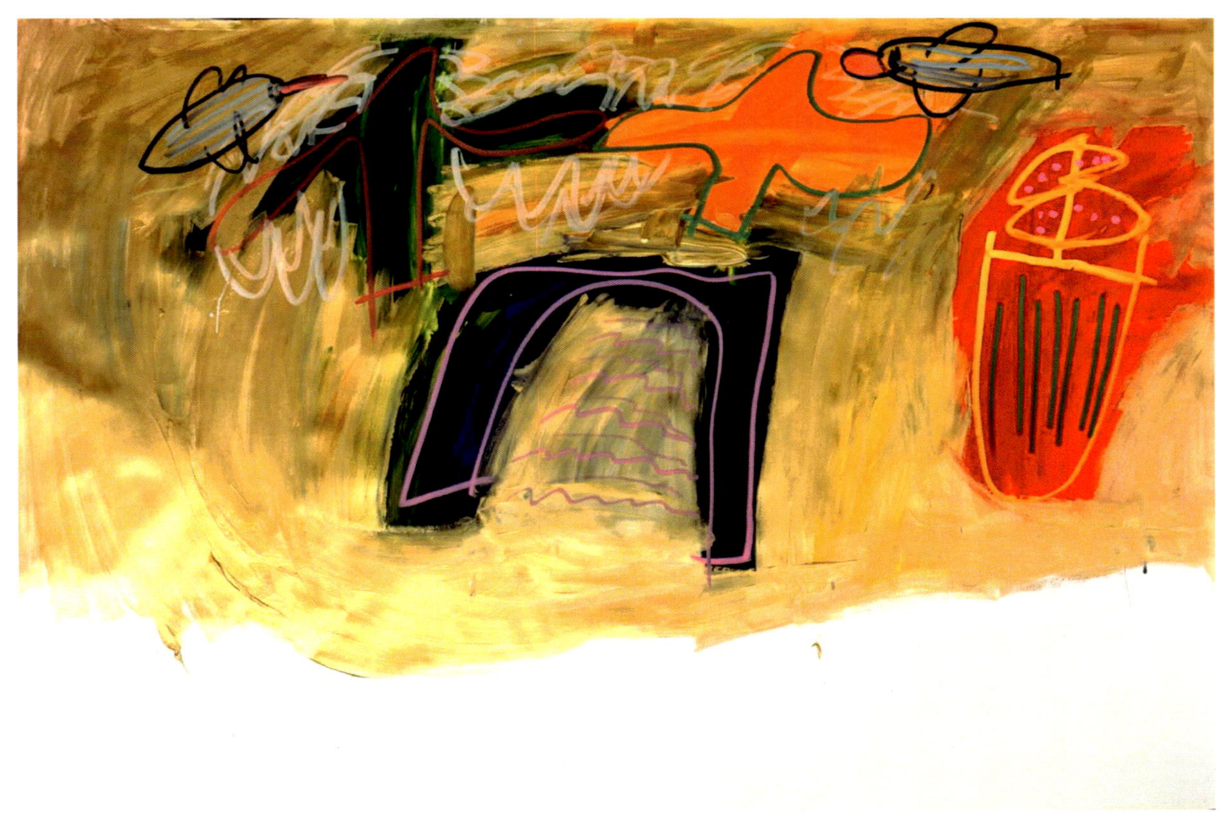

Villa with Birds
Painted on a Saturday afternoon in Brighton.
Acrylic on paper with added Posca pen, 2017, 151cm x 90cm.

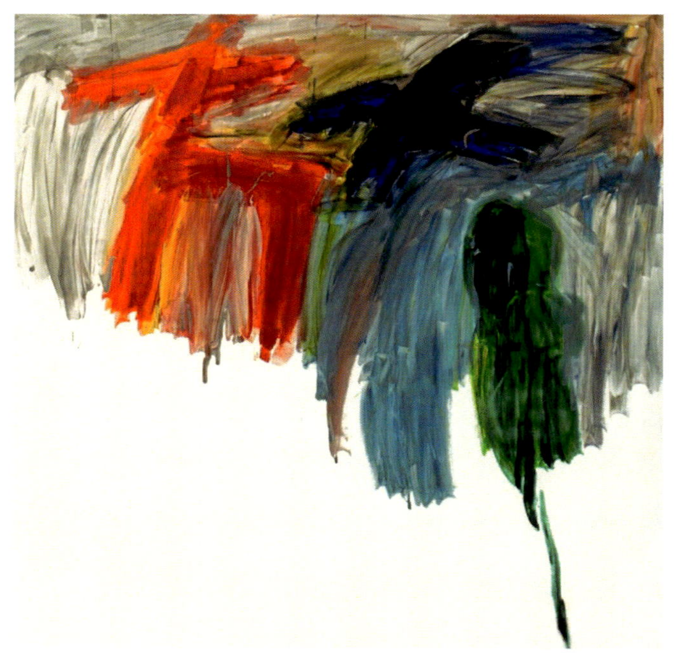

Villa and Pool
Saturday afternoon painting.
Acrylic on paper, 2017.

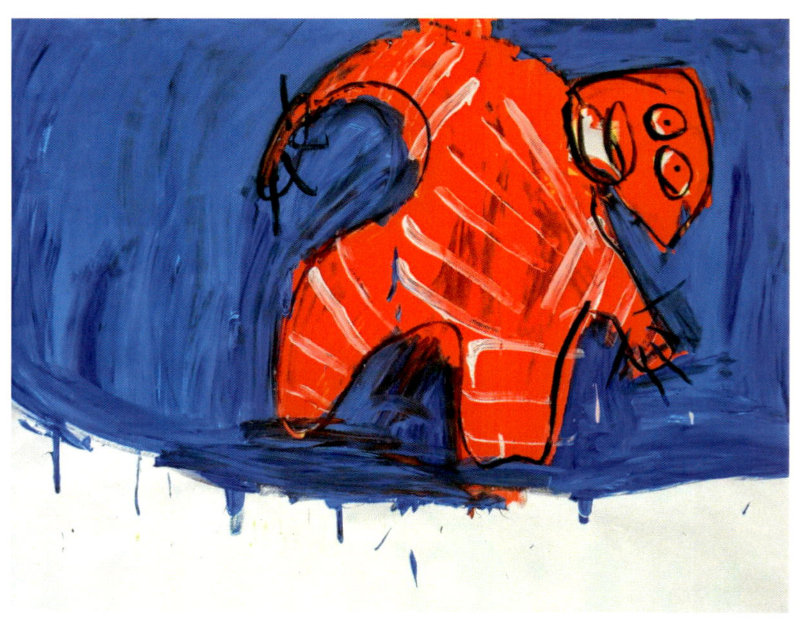

David Bowie
Copy of a photograph on the iPad.
Acrylic on paper, 2017, 151cm x 112cm.

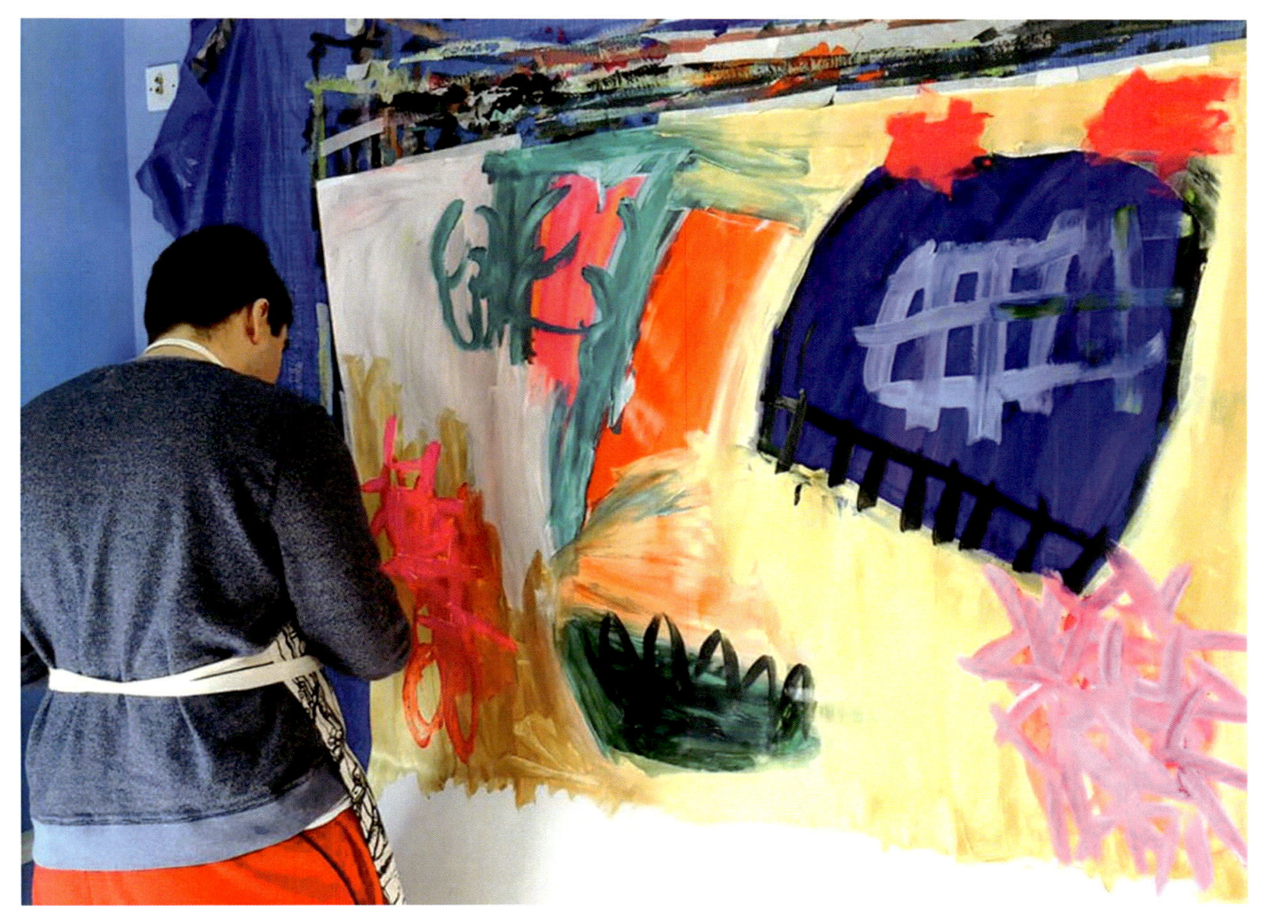

Johnny painting *House and Garden.* Inspired by David Hockney's painting *Garden* (2015). Acrylic on paper, 2017, 145cm x 125cm.

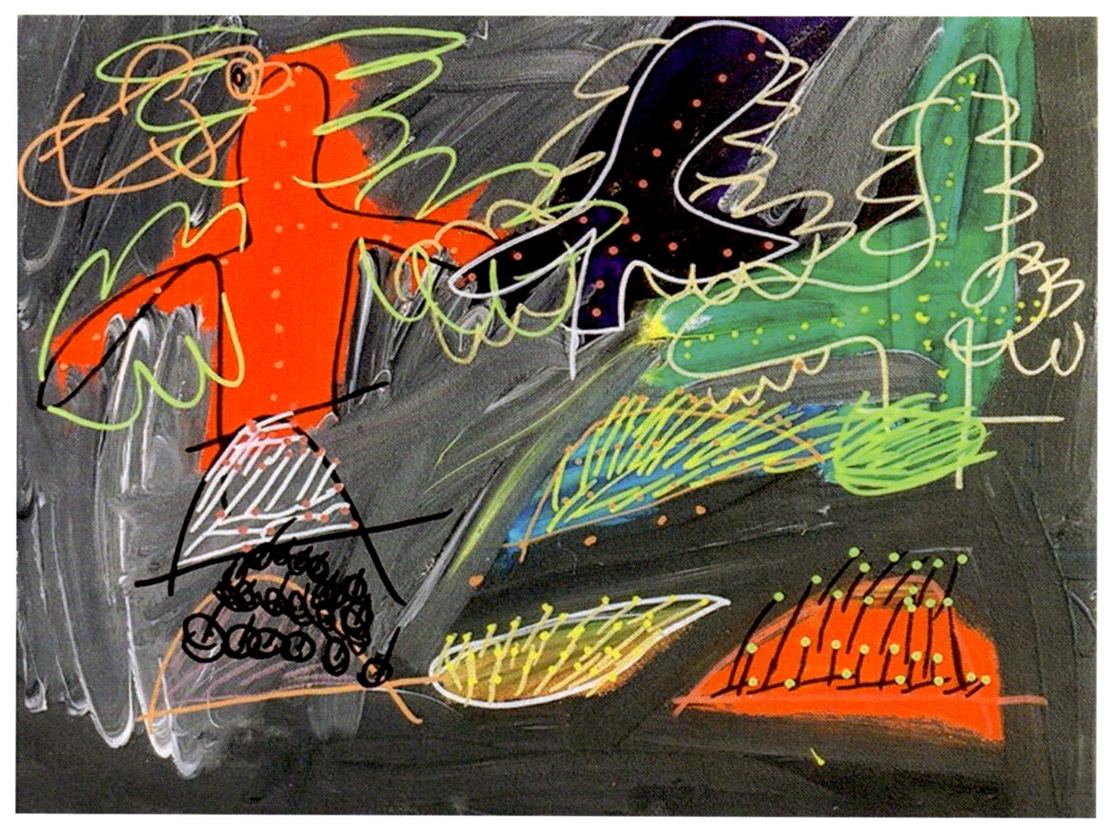

Cactus Tree
Painted in Portugal.
Acrylic on canvas board, 2017.

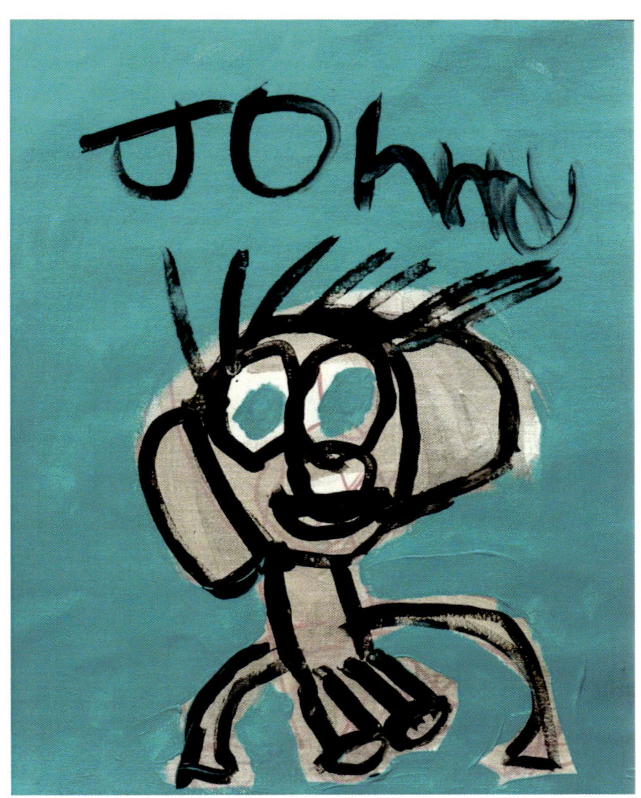

Self-Portrait
Painted in Portugal.
Acrylic on canvas paper, 2016, 40cm x 50cm.

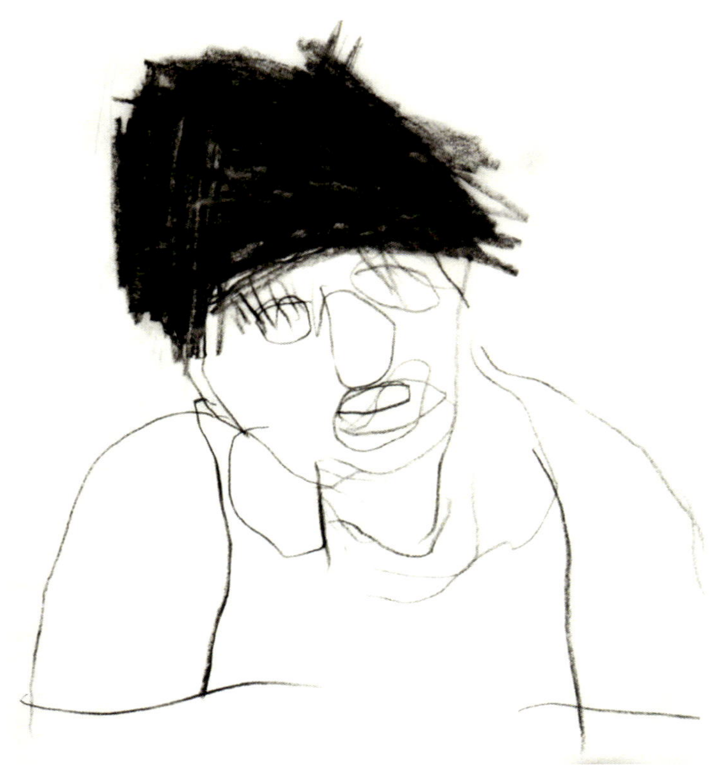

Black and White Self-Portrait
Stencilling over a photo on tracing paper using crayon
at Mymarc Art Club.
2016, 16cm x 18cm.

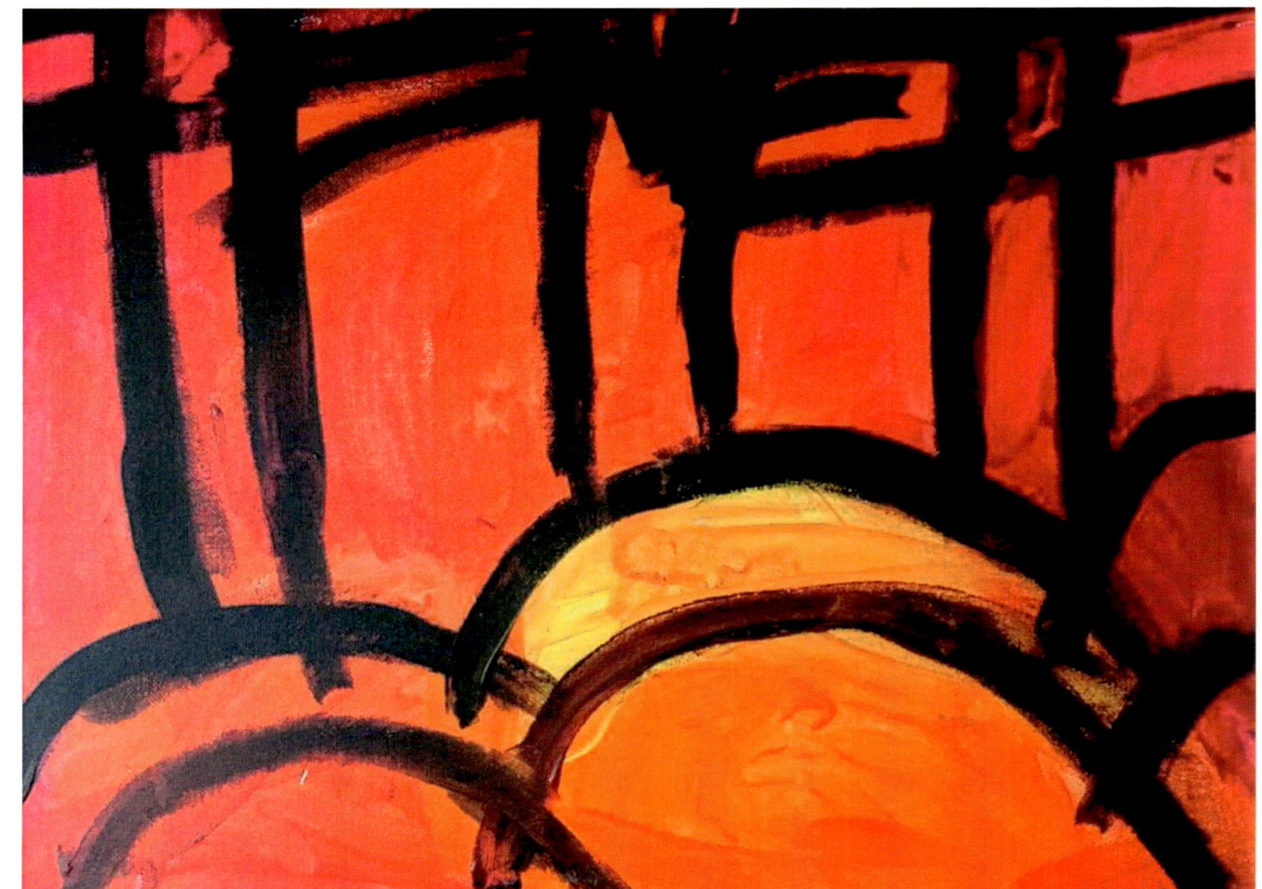

*Red and Orange
Hills and Trees*
This was Johnny's
first 'commission'
for a friend who
wanted a painting
in these colours.
Acrylic on canvas
board.

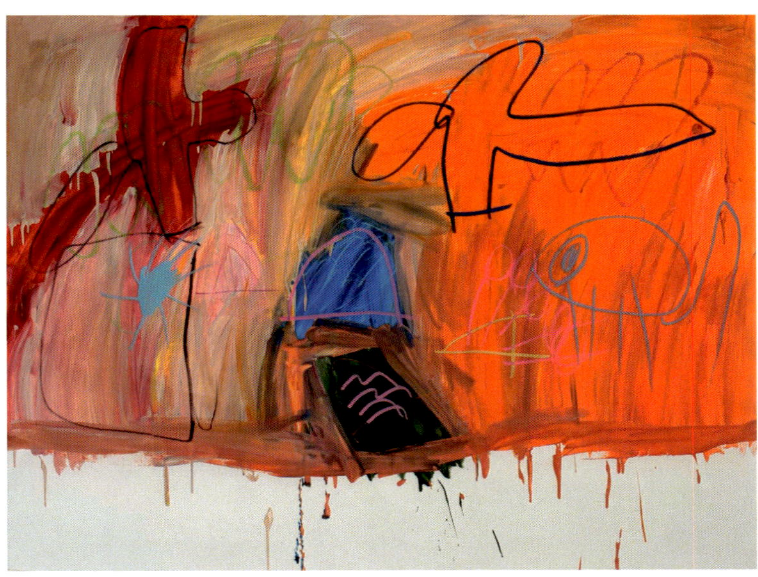

Hills and Trees with Bird and Horse.
Acrylic on paper with added Posca pen,
151cm x 108cm.

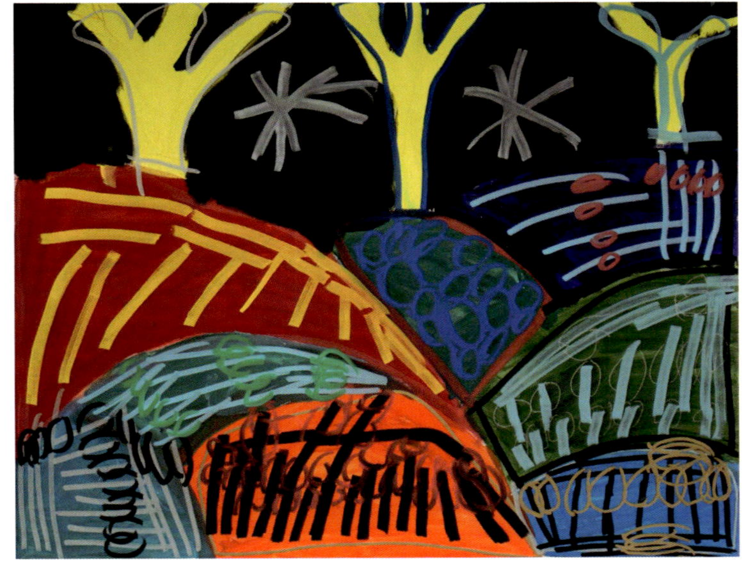

Revisiting an early *Hills and Trees* with Posca pen, 2017.

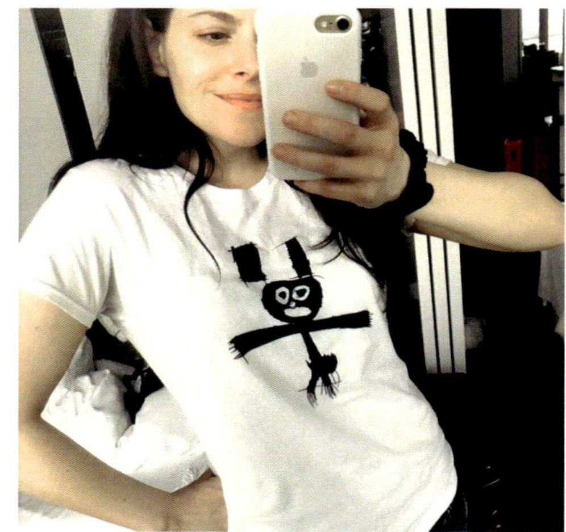

Emily Hampshire modelling her
Kung Fu Panda T-shirt, 2017.

I wish I could perfectly articulate what makes Johnny's work so special because he is truly my favourite artist. Everything about his work feels so pure and authentic. I'm in love with his art but it's such a hard thing for me to explain the 'why' of. I guess because it's honest and therefore touches something deep in me that is true but not expressed.

Emily Hampshire
Actress

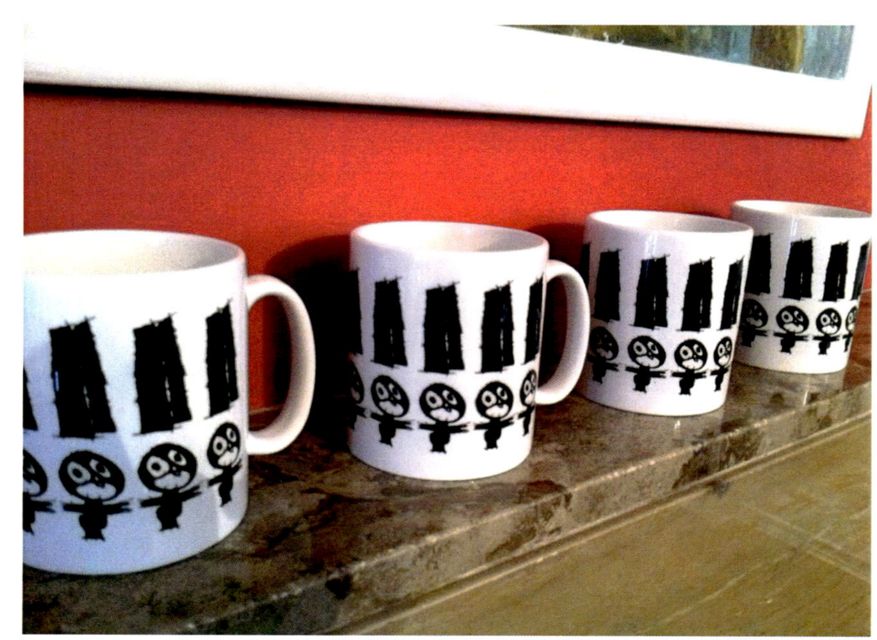

Black and white *Kung Fu Panda* figures printed on mugs, c.2013.

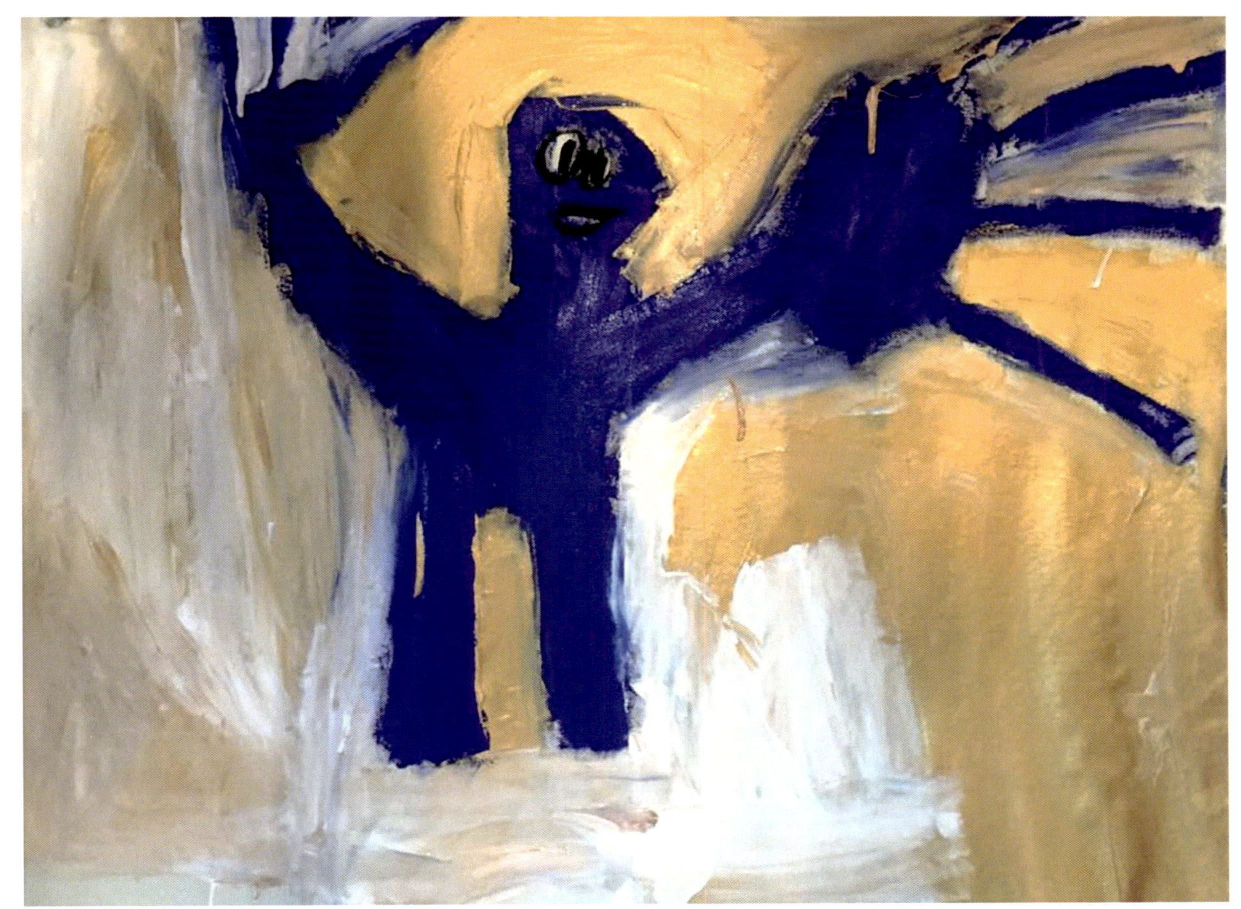

Blue Man
Acrylic on untreated
canvas, 2017.

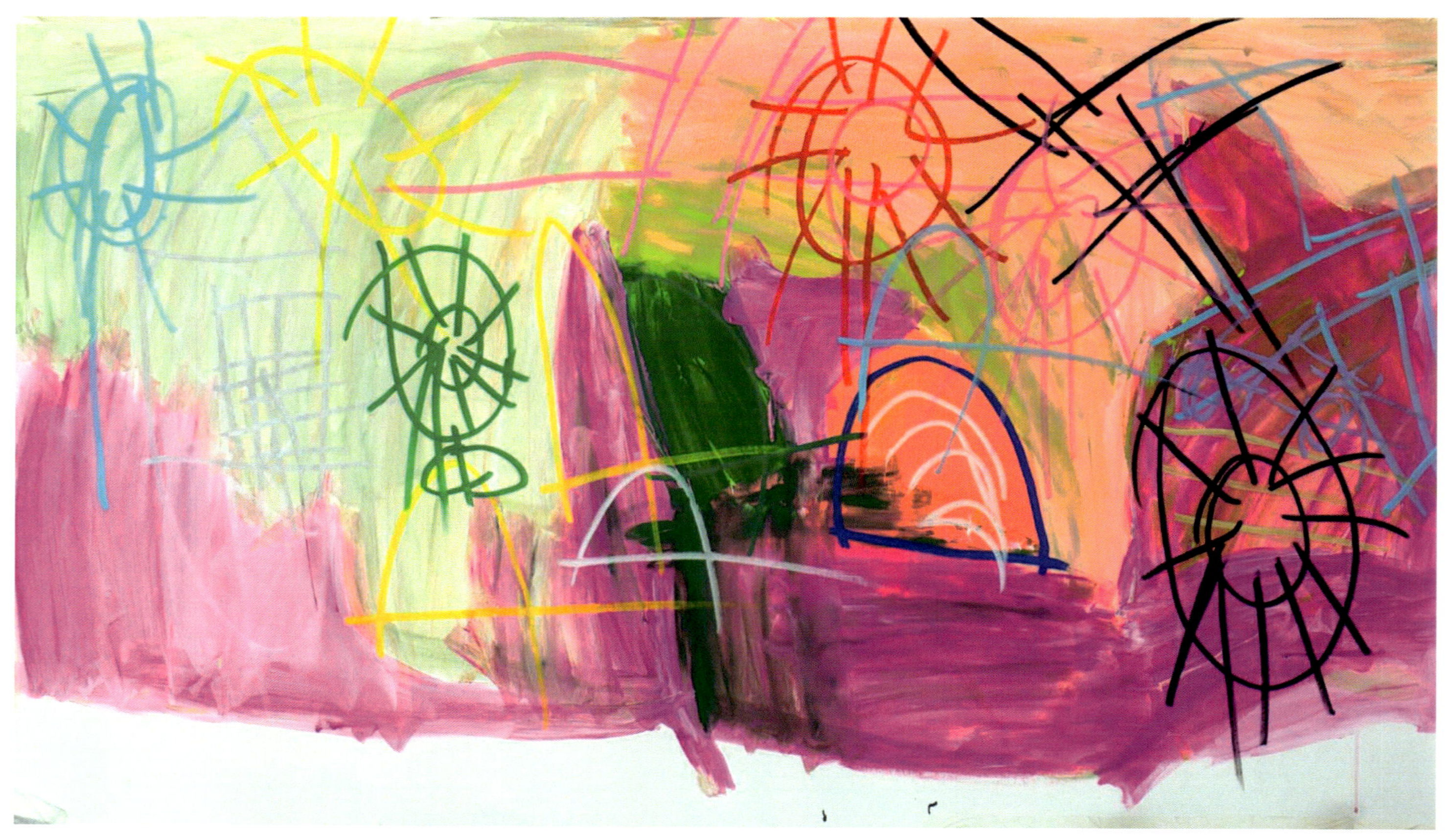

Flowers
Acrylic on paper with Posca pen, 2016, 151cm x 87cm.

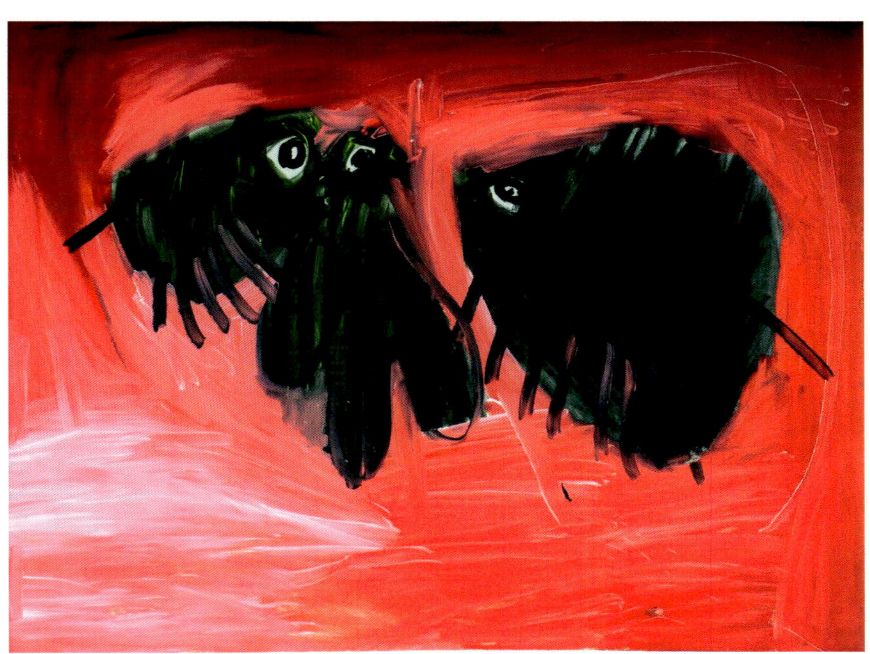

Dido and her Horses
Painted at Rocket Artists Studio.
Acrylic on canvas, 2017, 126cm x 96cm.

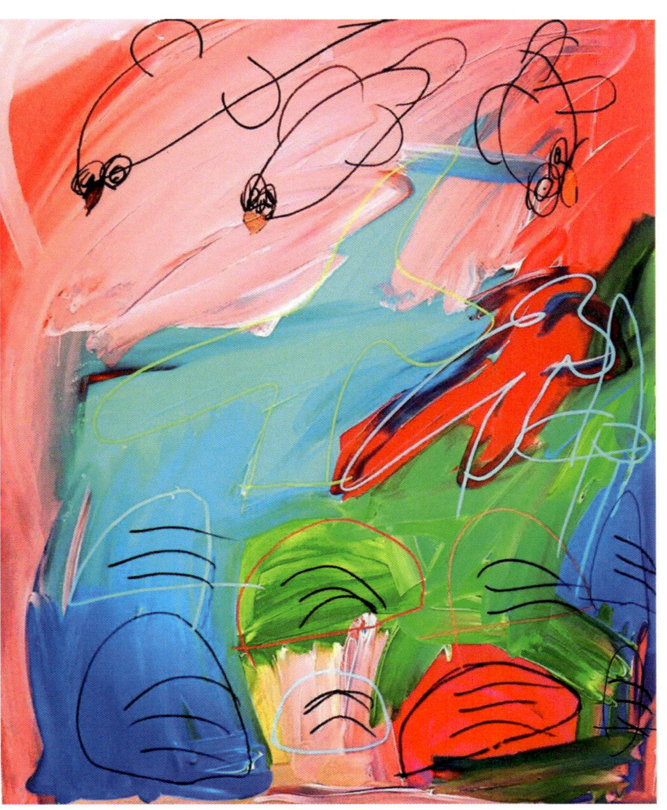

Hills, Trees and Seagulls
Painted in Portugal.
Acrylic on canvas with added Posca pen, 2016.

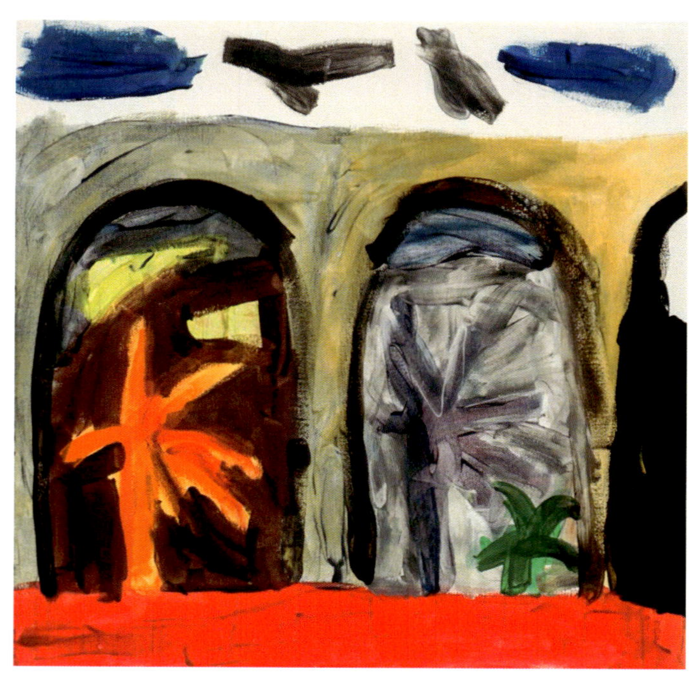

View from Villa
Acrylic on canvas, c.2008, 50cm x 50cm.

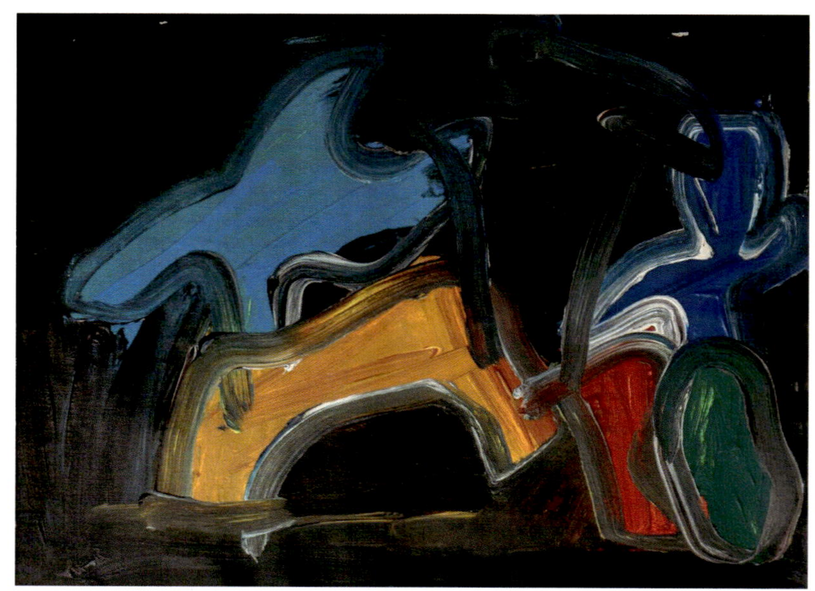

Villa and Pool at Night
Painted in Portugal.
Acrylic on canvas, 2016.

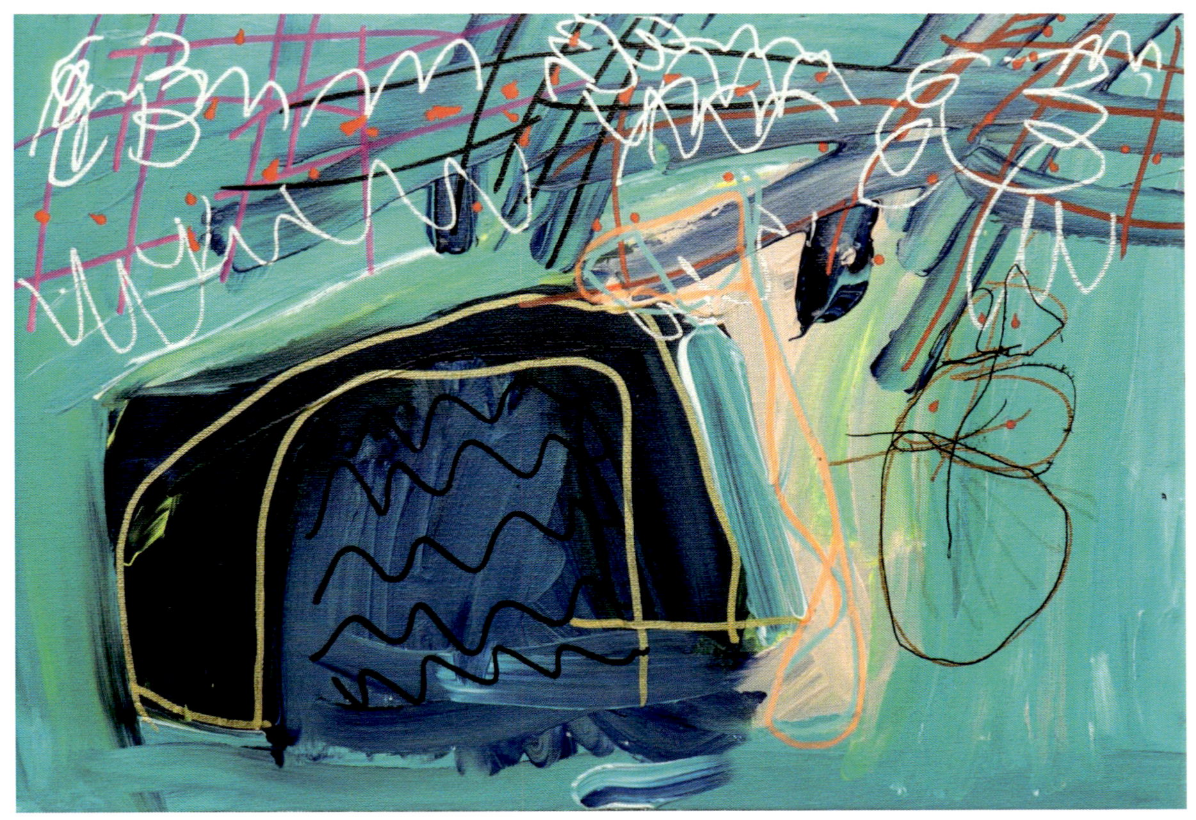

Villa, Pool and Pot Plant
Painted in Portugal.
Acrylic on canvas board with added Posca pen, 2017, 41cm x 30cm.

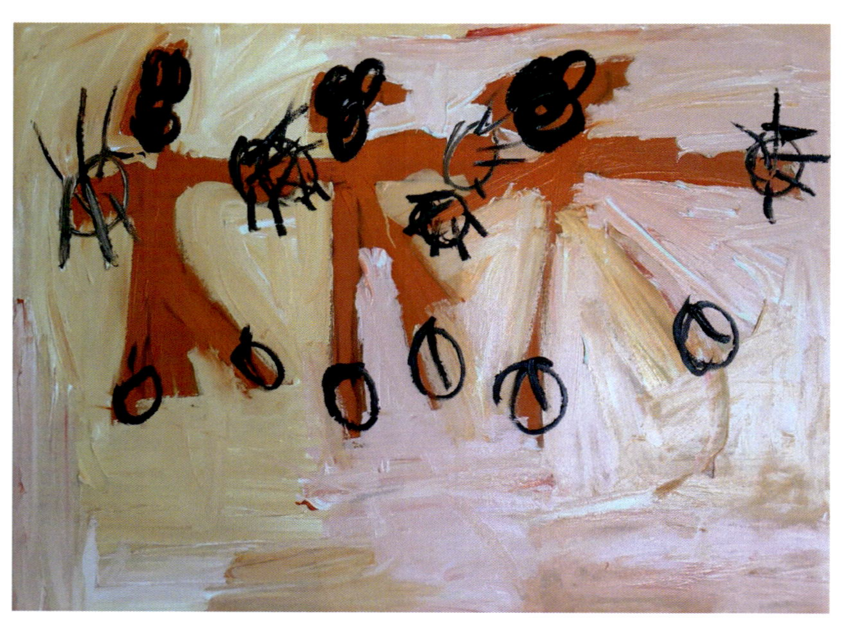

Johnny and Parents
Painted at Rocket Artists Studio.
Acrylic on canvas, 2017.

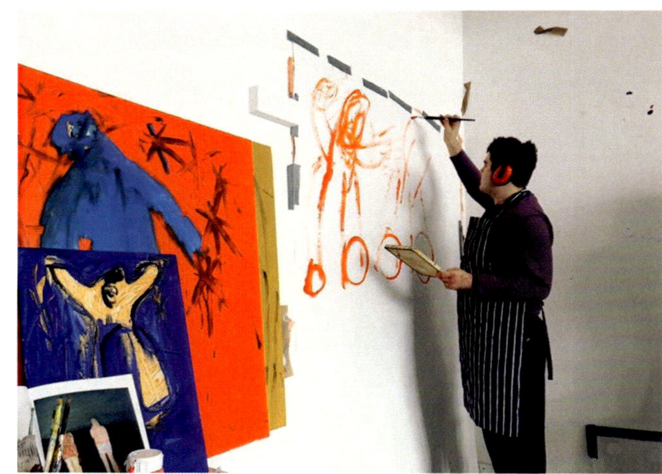

Johnny starting a picture at The Rocket Artists Studio.
Inspired by Tom Hammick's painting *Field* (2003).
The other paintings are the work Johnny had done
in the previous week's session.

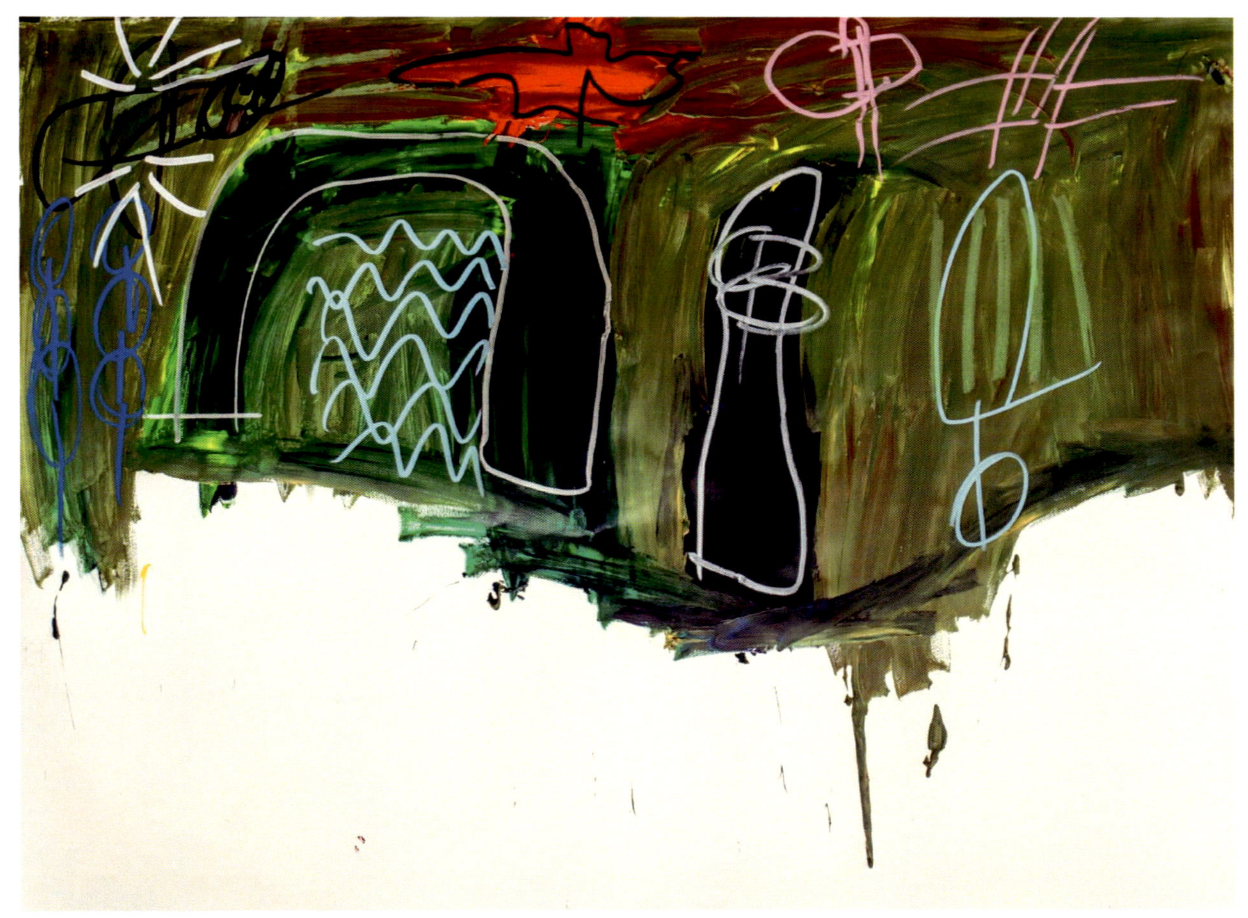

Villa and Pool
Acrylic on paper with
added Posca pen, 2017,
151cm x 114cm.

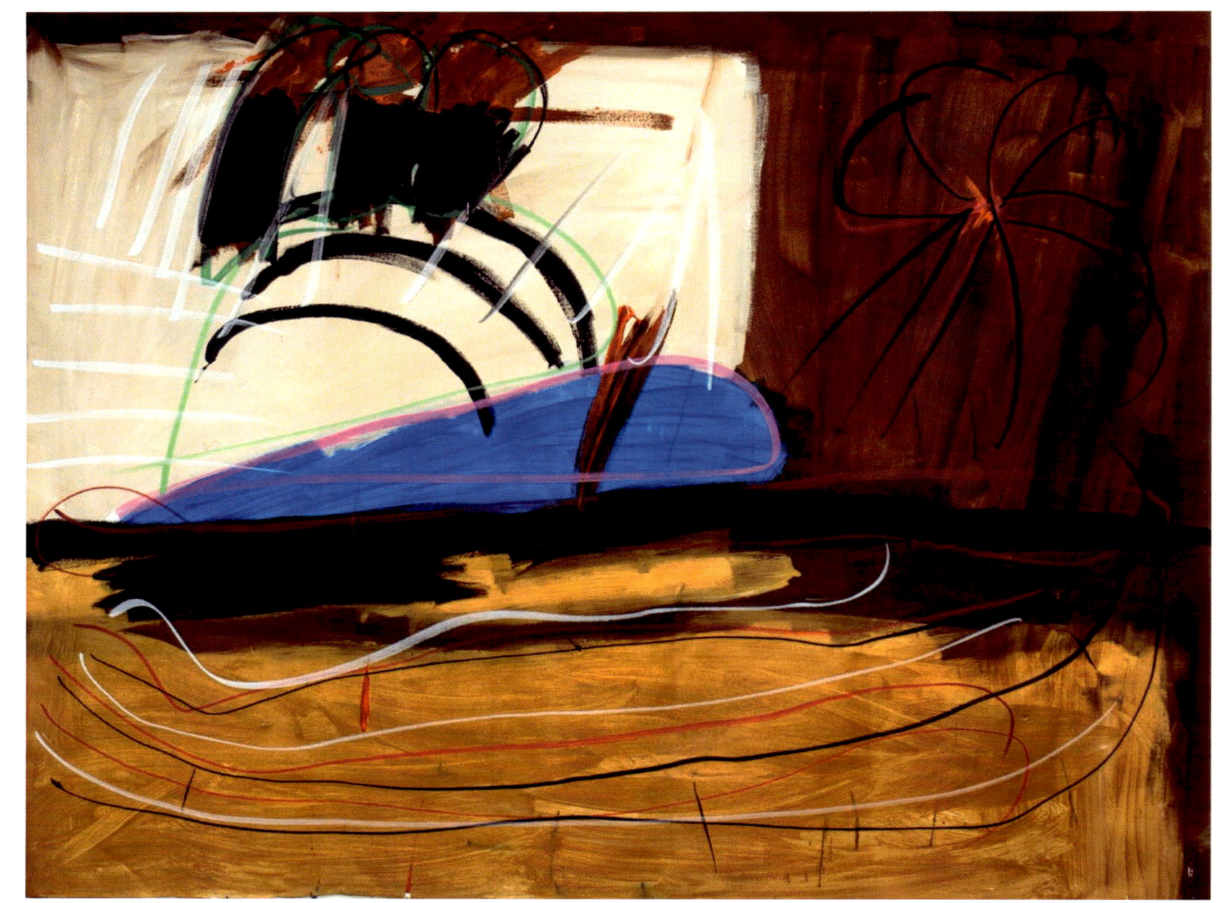

Three Trees on a Hill
Acrylic on large
canvas, 2016,
162cm x 128cm.

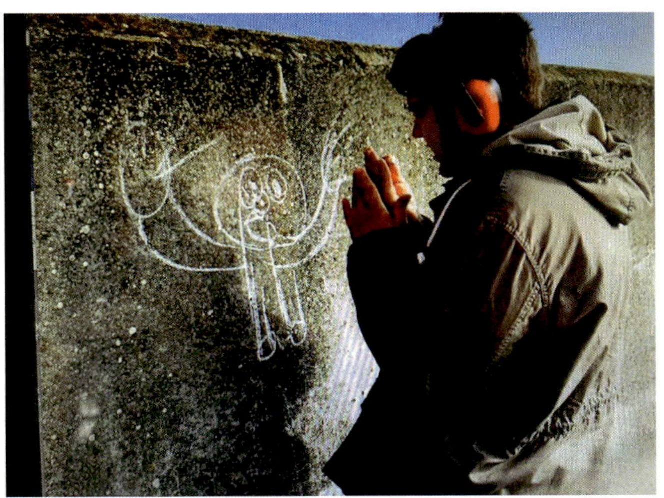

Johnny doing chalk graffiti at
Ovingdean Beach, 2015.

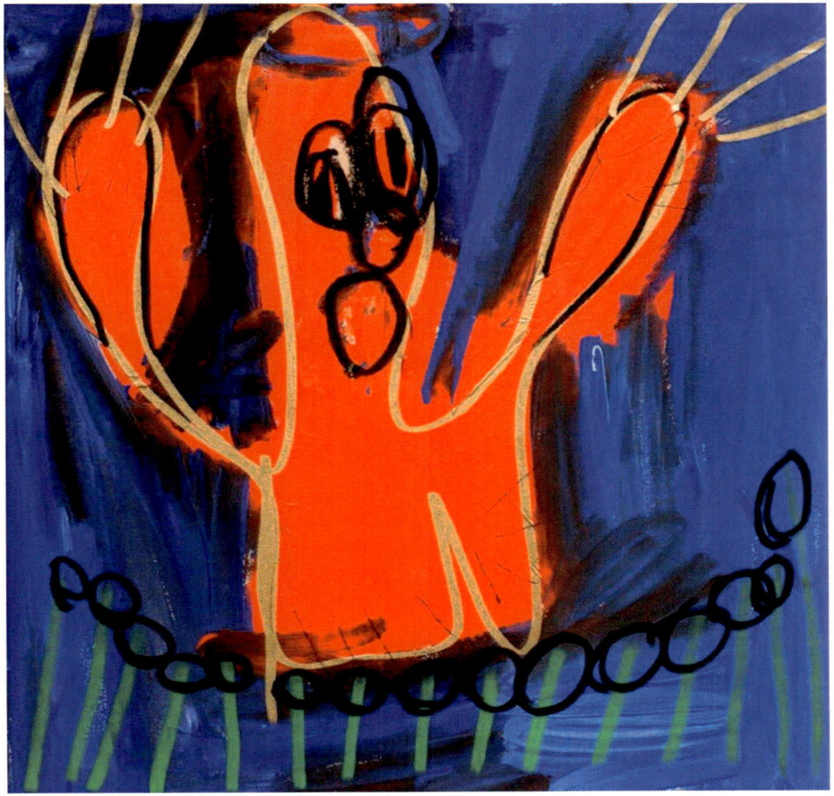

Red Man
Acrylic on canvas with added Posca pen,
2017, 60cm x 60cm.

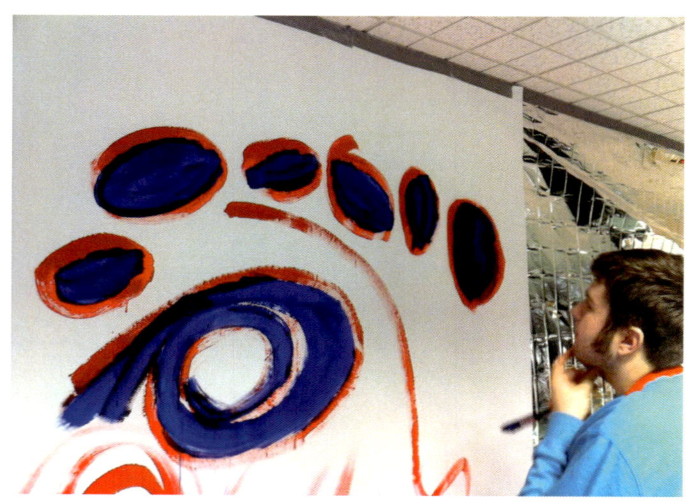

Johnny painting a fish at Mymarc Art group, 2015.

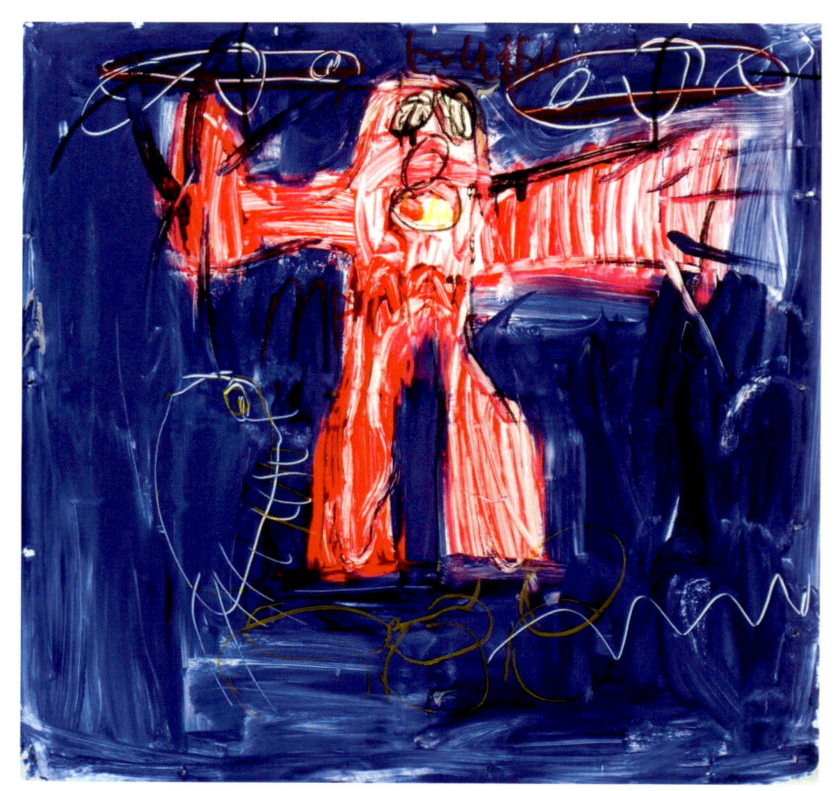

Red Man with Creatures
Acrylic on clear plastic sheeting, 2017.

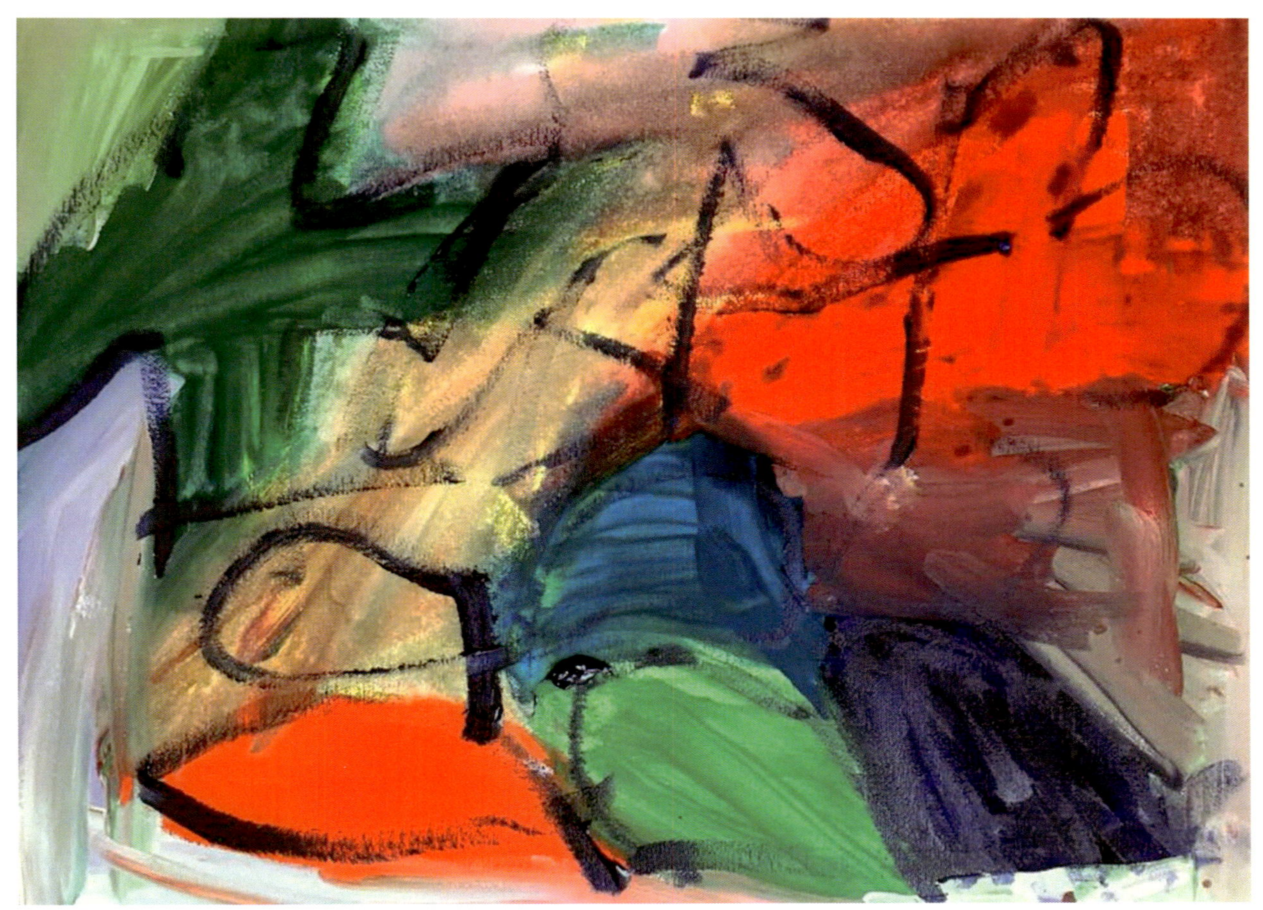

Hills and Trees
Watercolour on
canvas board,
c.2015.

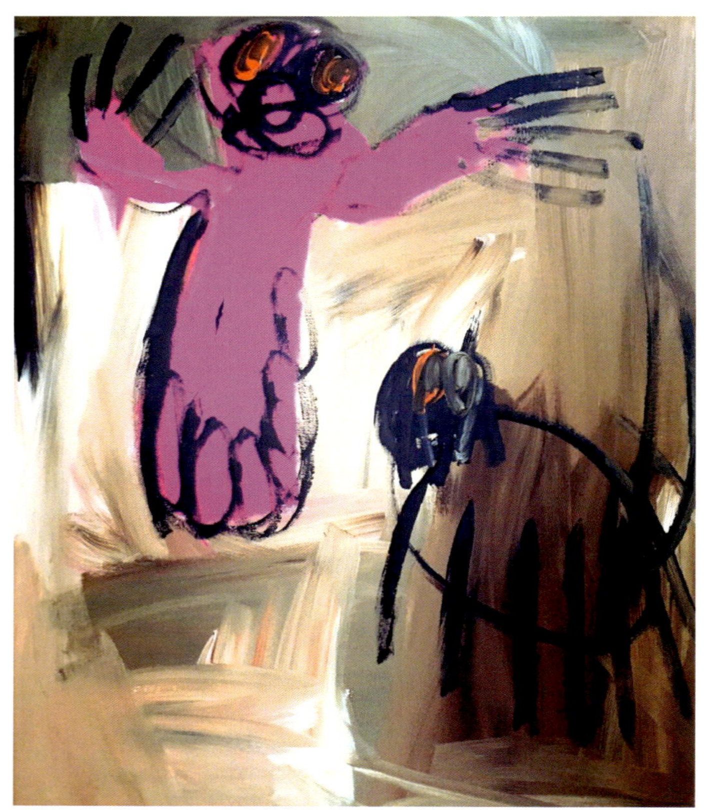

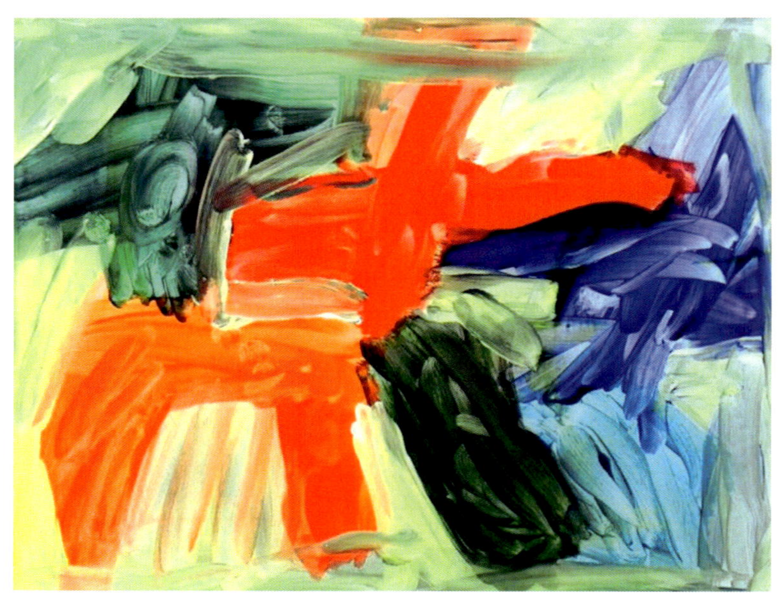

Villa and Pool
Watercolour on paper, 2017.

Pink Man and Dog
Painted at Rocket Artists Studio.
Acrylic on canvas, 2017, 94cm x 126cm.

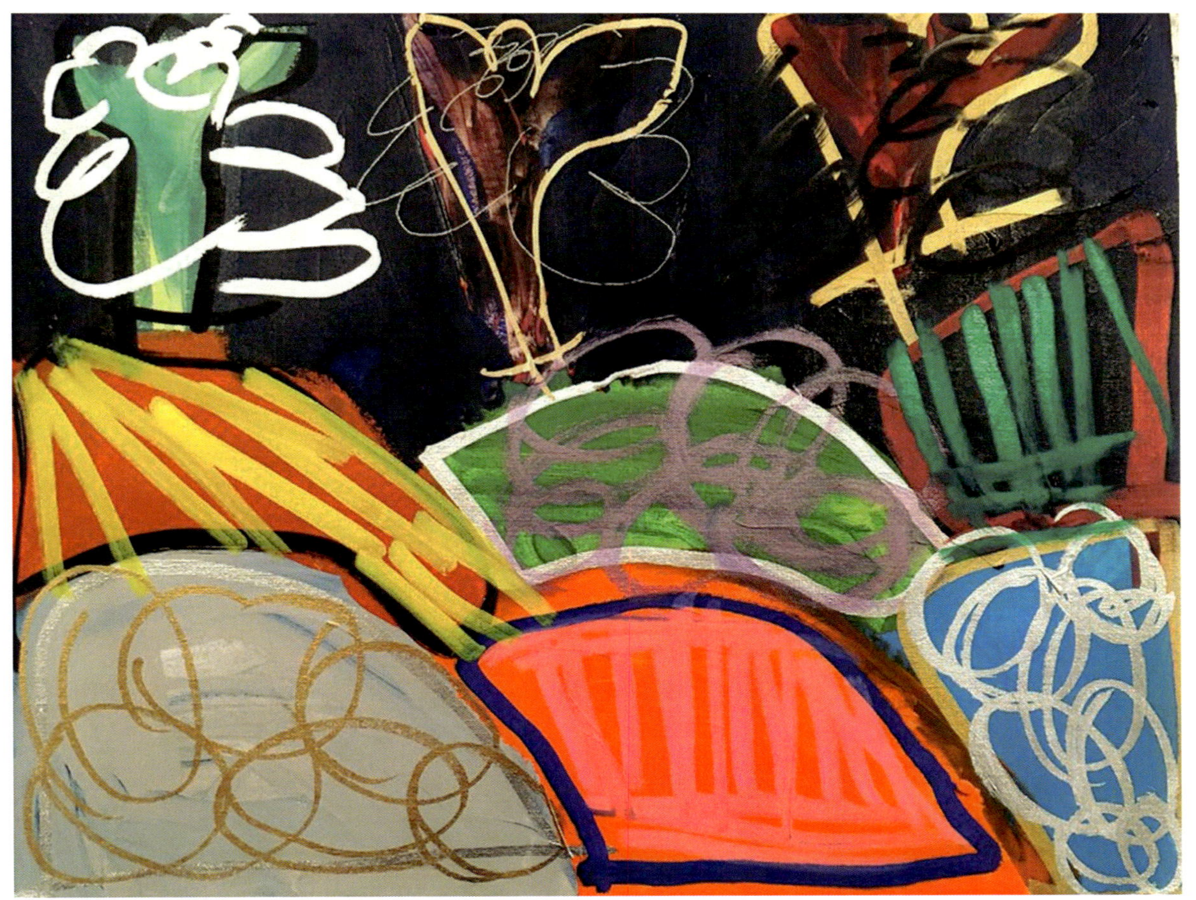

Hills and Trees
Acrylic on canvas
with added Posca,
2017, 50cm x 40cm.

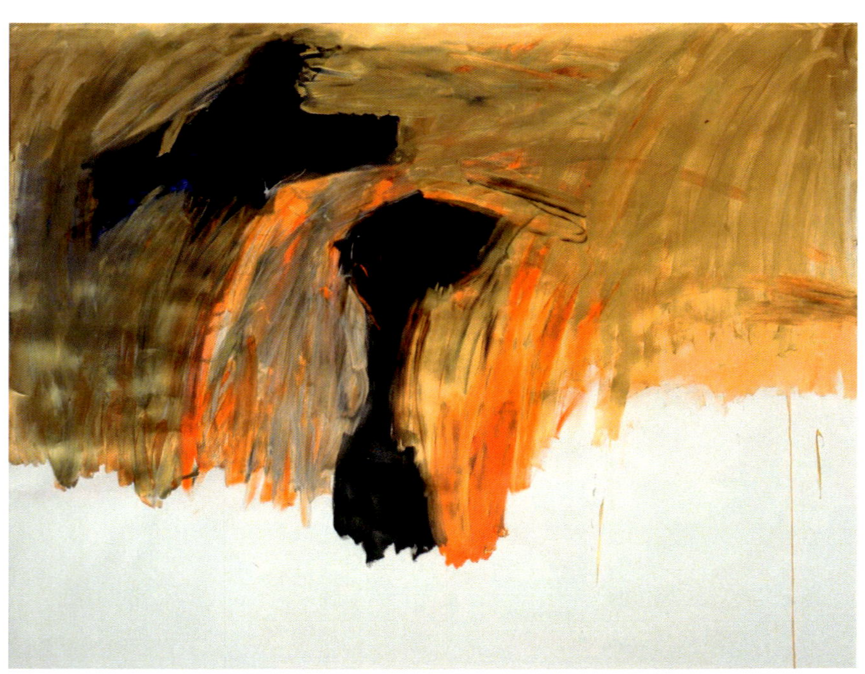

Villa and Pool
Acrylic on paper, 2016, 151cm x 117cm.

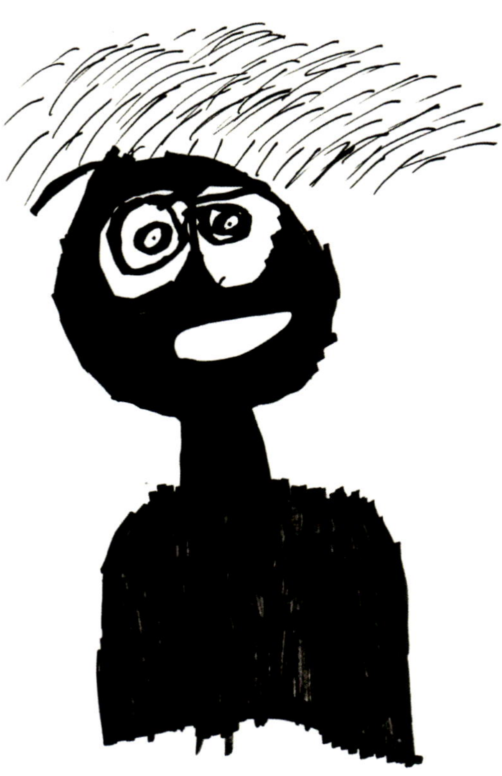

Black and White Self-Portrait
Permanent marker on paper,
2016, 40cm x 55cm.

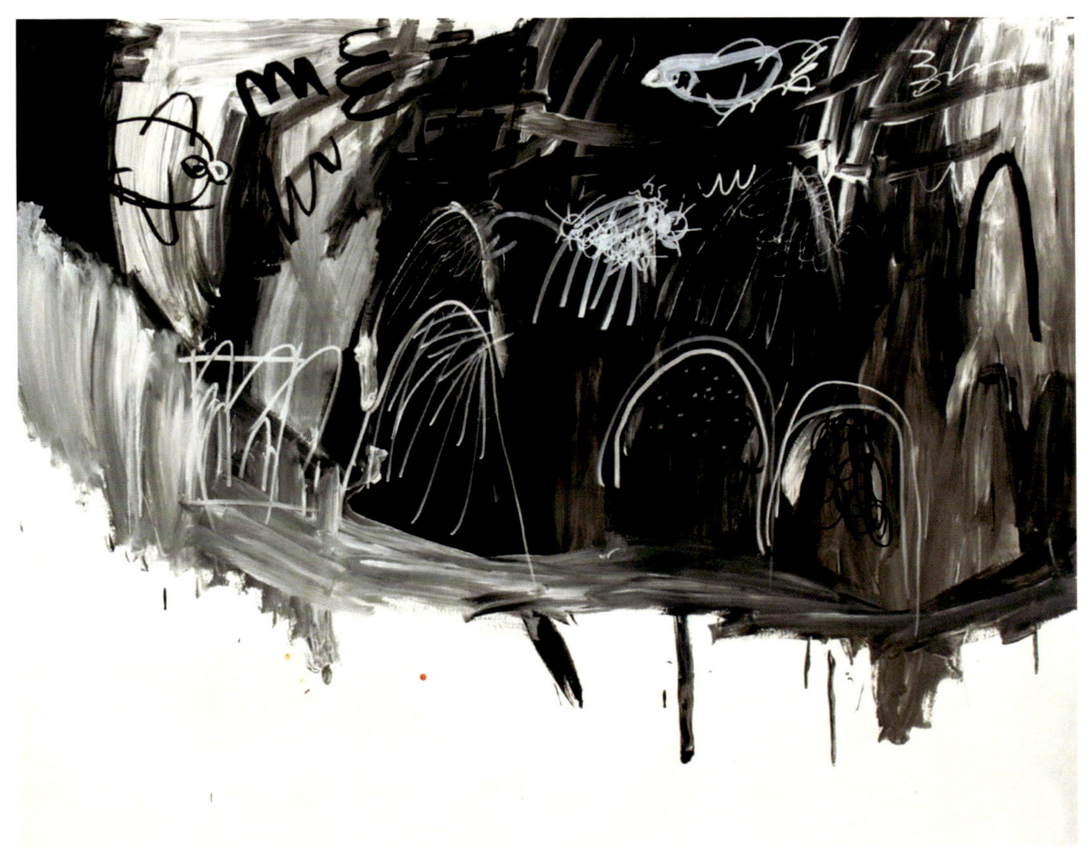

Black and White Experiment: Hills and Trees
Acrylic on paper with added Posca, Halloween 2017, 151cm x 115cm.

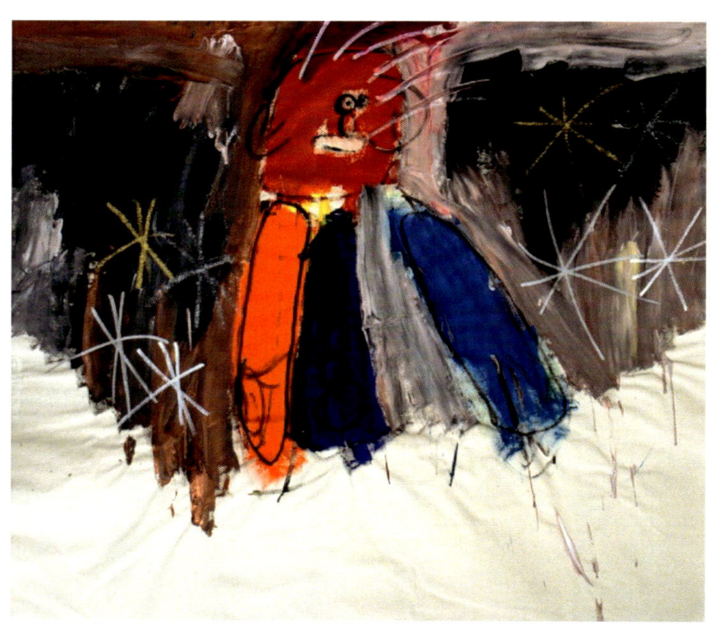

Painting inspired by Miro's *Autorretrato* (1919).
Acrylic on untreated canvas with added Posca pen,
2017, 149cm x 112cm.

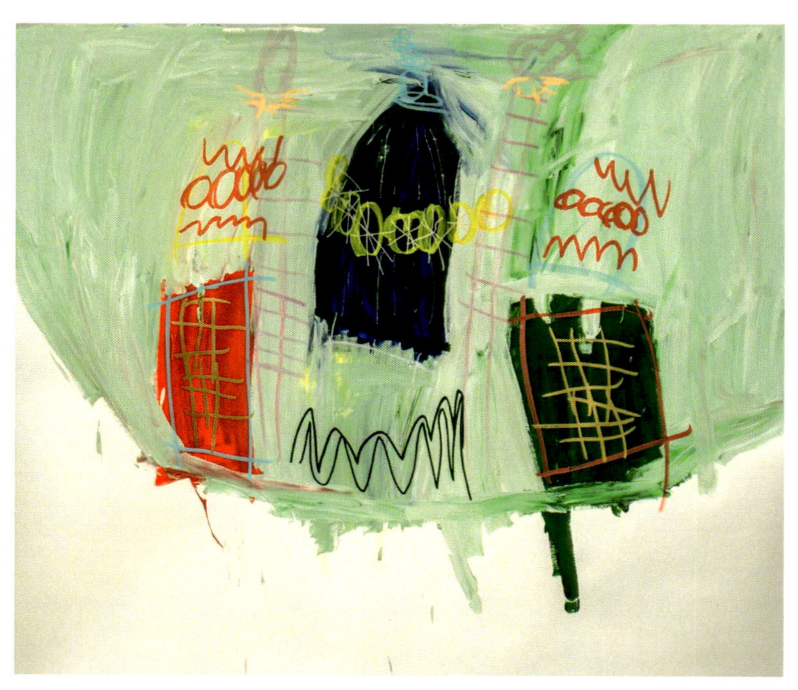

Brighton Pavilion
Acrylic on paper with added Posca pen,
2017, 151cm x 125cm.

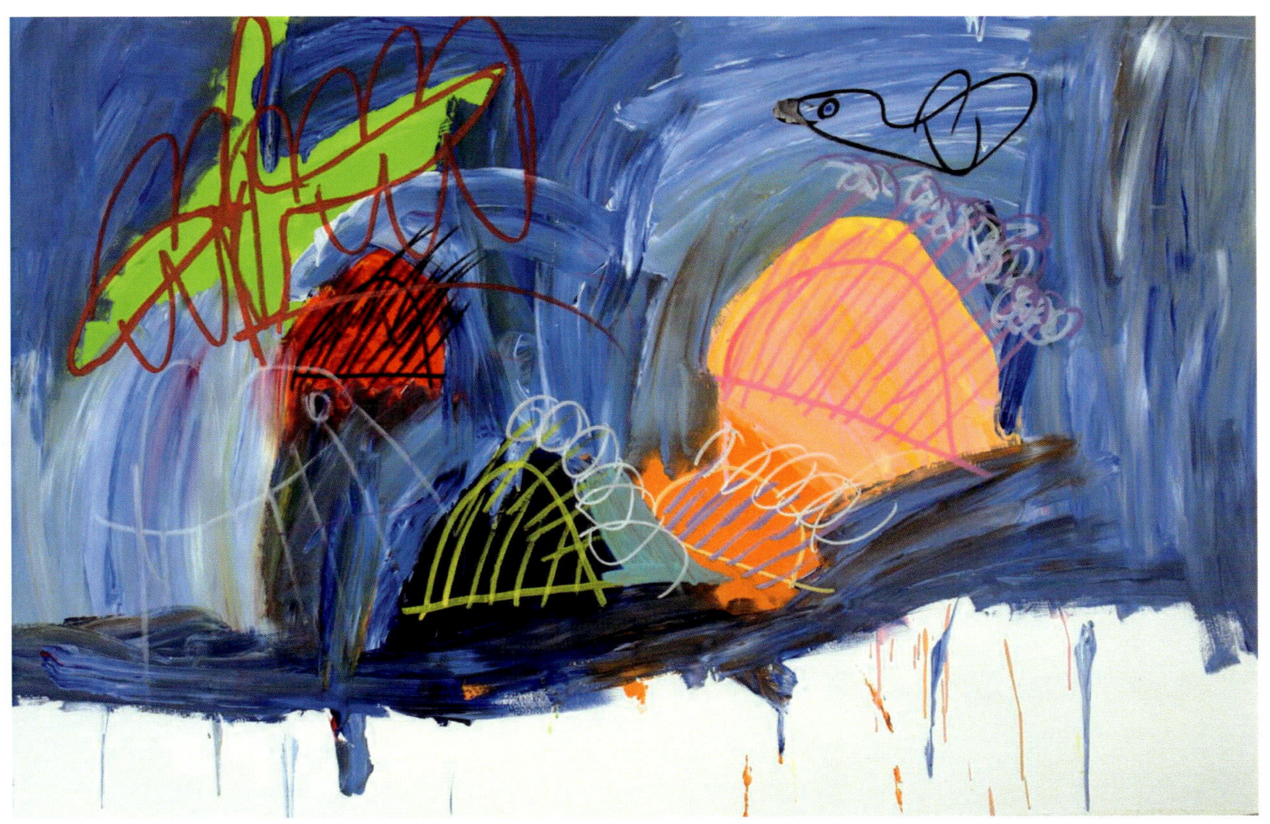

Hills and Trees with Bird and Horse
Acrylic on paper with added Posca pen,
2017, 151cm x 102cm.

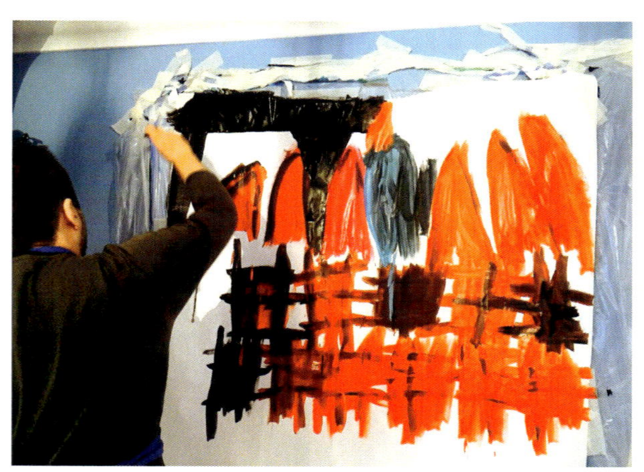

Johnny painting Brighton Pavilion.

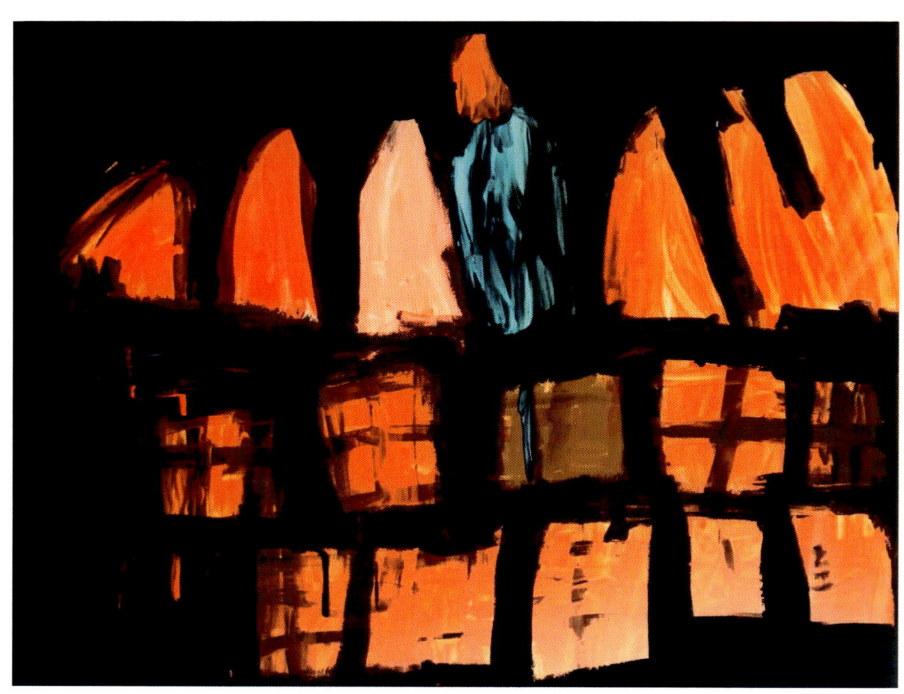

Brighton Pavilion
Acrylic on paper, 2015, 65cm x 50cm.

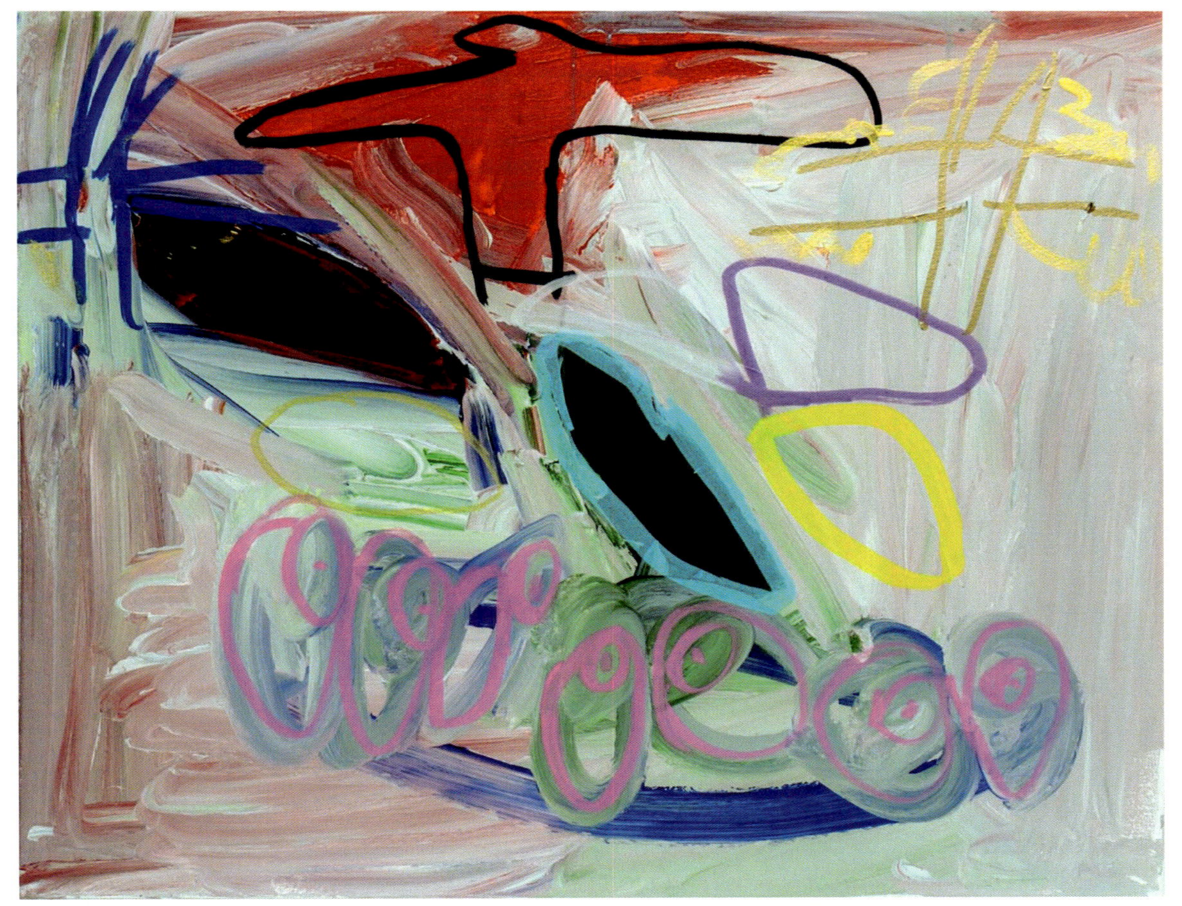

Ducks on the Lake
Painted at Sacred
Earth Land Project
in Horam.
Acrylic on canvas,
2017.

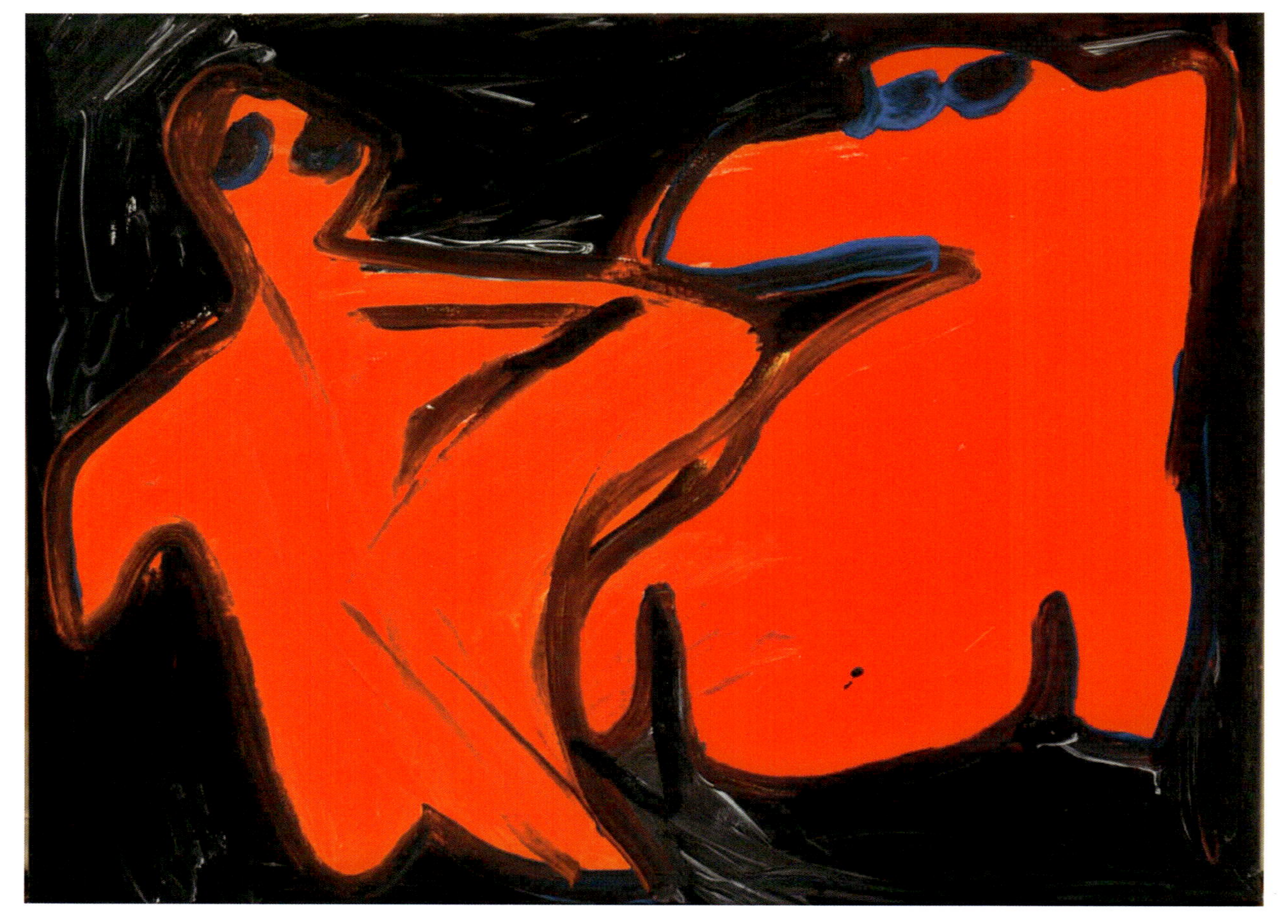

Two Red Figures
Acrylic on
canvas, 2016,
60cm x 46cm.

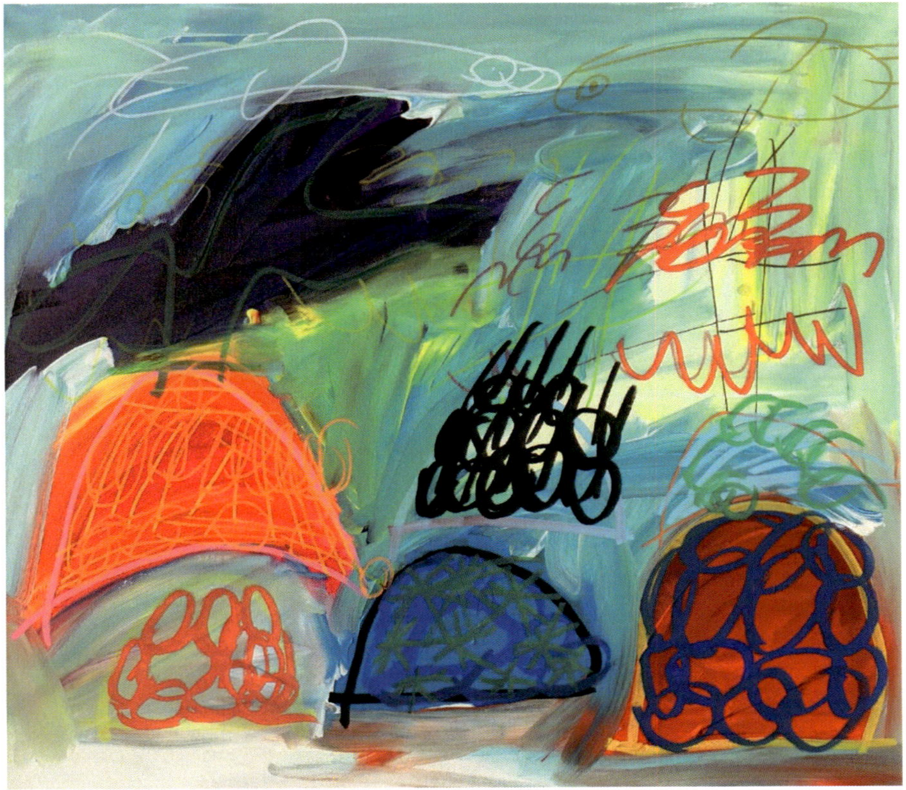

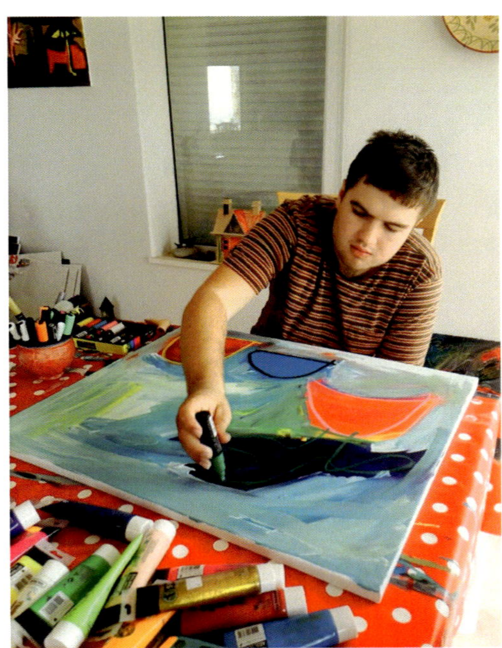

Johnny adding Posca pen to a
Hills and Trees painting.

Hills and Trees
Painted in Portugal.
Acrylic on canvas with added Posca, 2017.

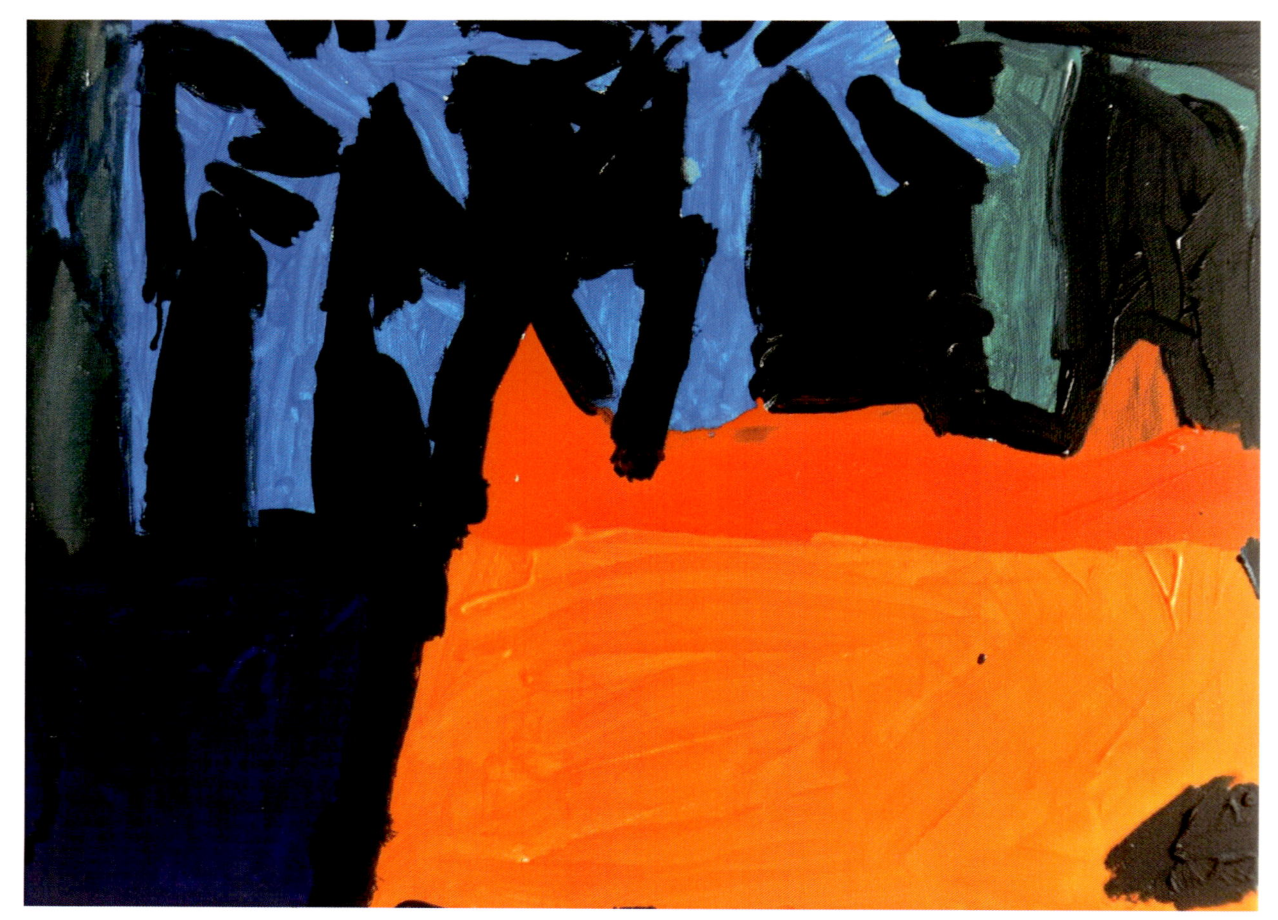

Villa and Pool
Acrylic on canvas
board, c.2009.

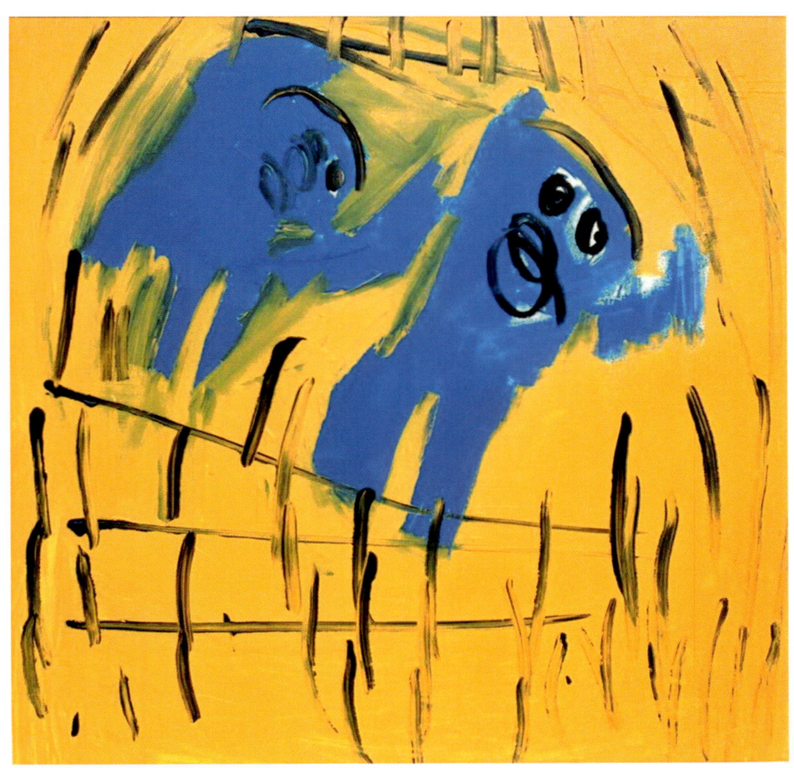

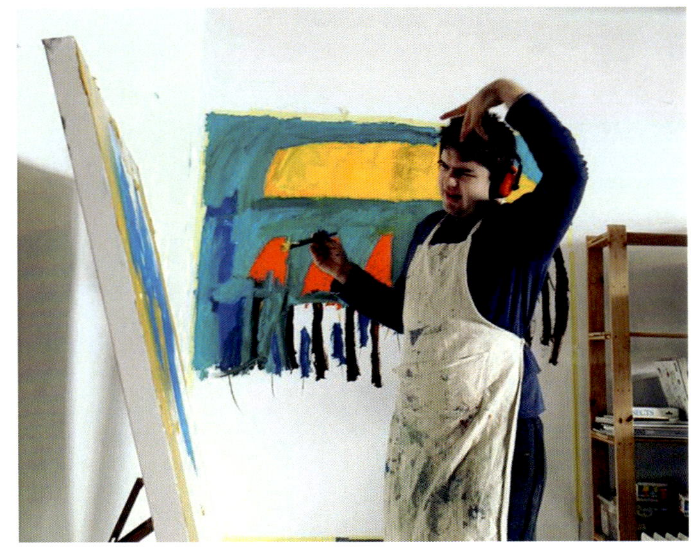

Johnny considering his painting of circus figures –
with his recent, unfinished painting of *Mountains*
in the background. Rocket Artists Studio, 2017.

Two Blue Figures on a Tightrope
Painted at Rocket Artists Studio.
Inspired by Maxwell Holyoke-Hirsch painting.
Acrylic on canvas, 2017, 97cm x 97cm.

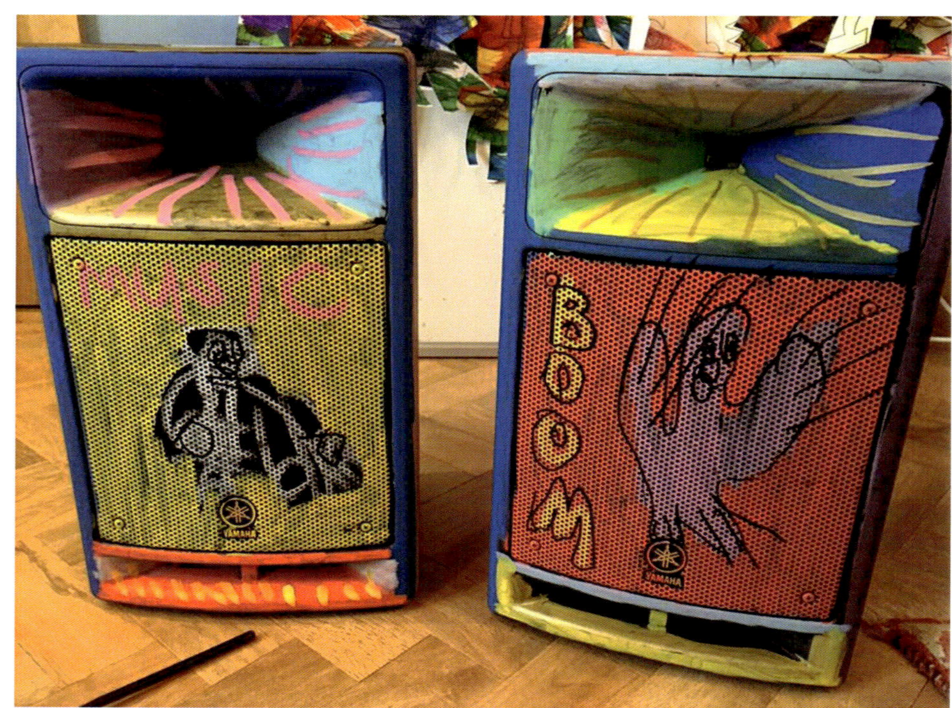

Front of hand-painted speakers by Johnny.
Posca pens, 2016.

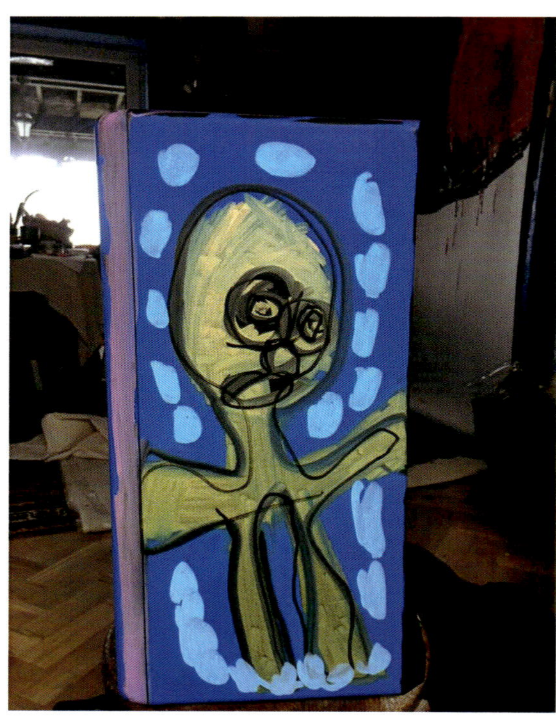

Side of hand-painted speakers by Johnny.
Posca pens, 2016.

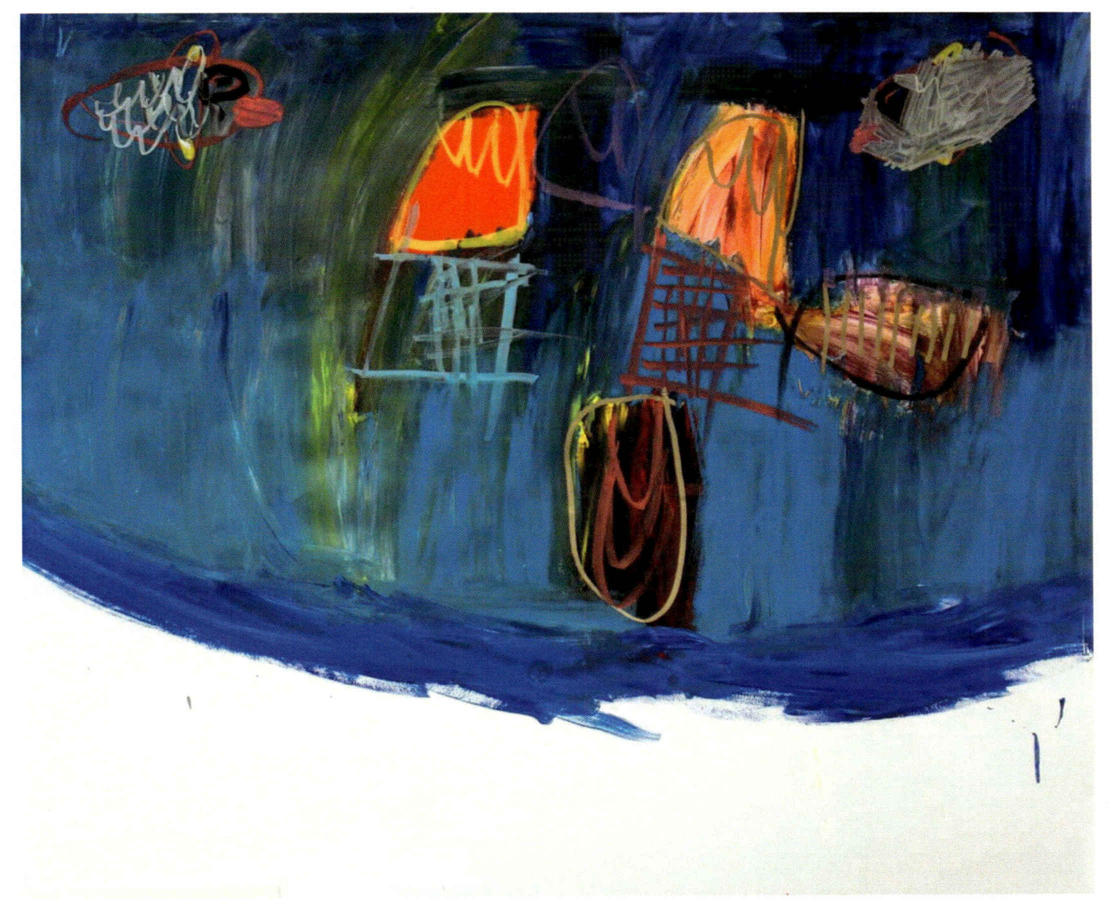

*Brighton Pavilion
with Seagulls*
Acrylic on paper
with added Posca
and glitter pen, 2017,
151cm x 117cm.

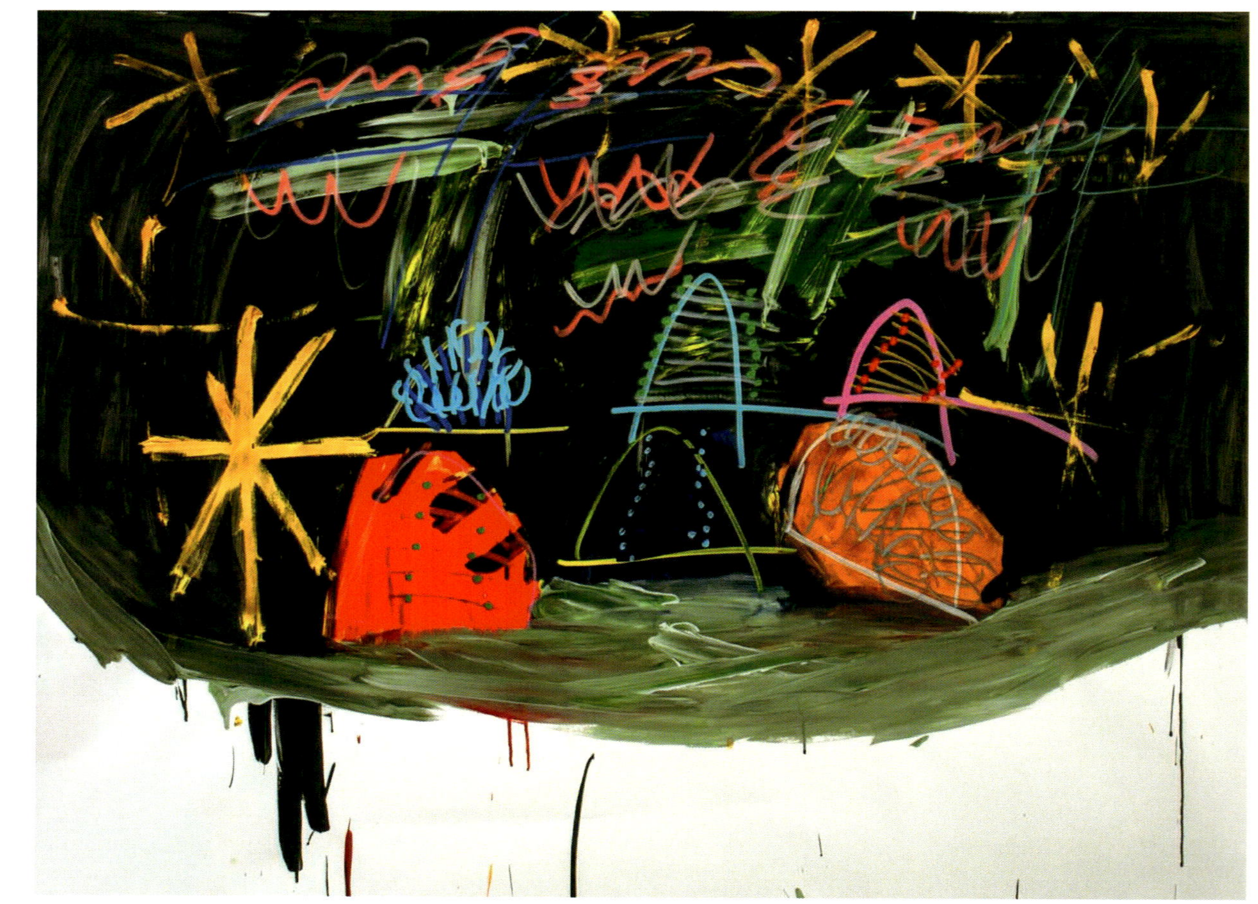

Hills and Trees at Night
Acrylic on paper with
added Posca pen and
gold paint, 2017,
151cm x 115cm.

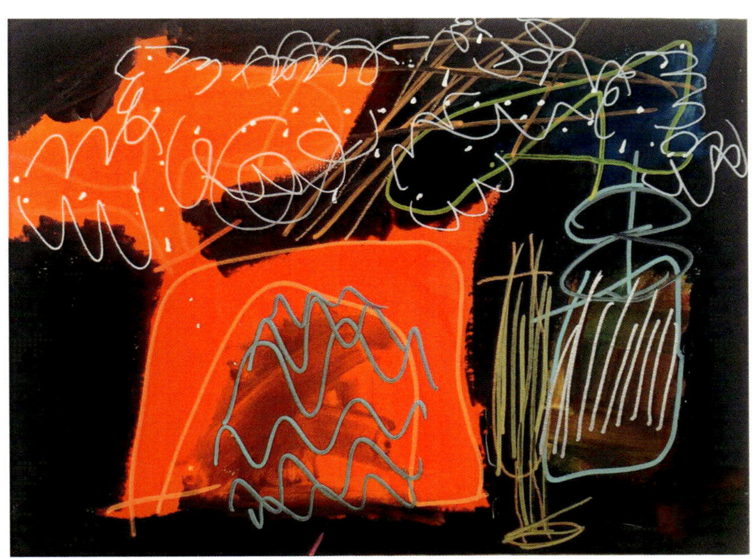

Villa and Pool
Painted in Portugal.
Acrylic on canvas board with added Posca, 2017.

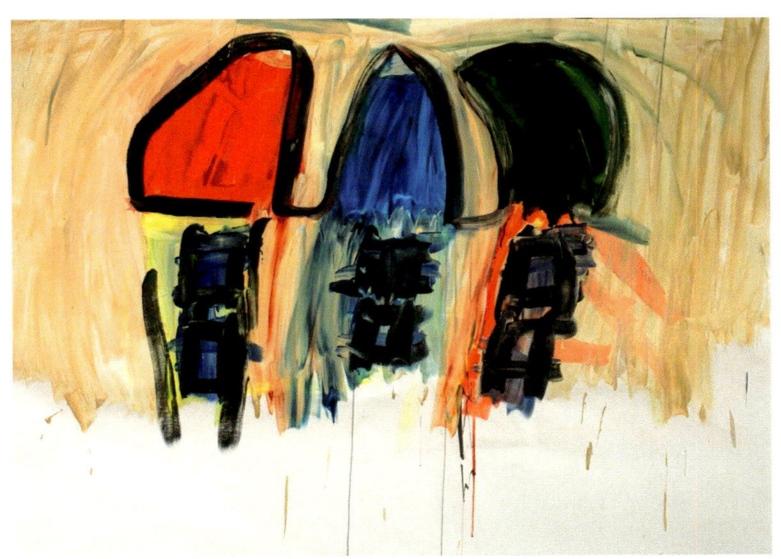

Brighton Pavilion
Acrylic on canvas, 2016, 151cm x 107cm.

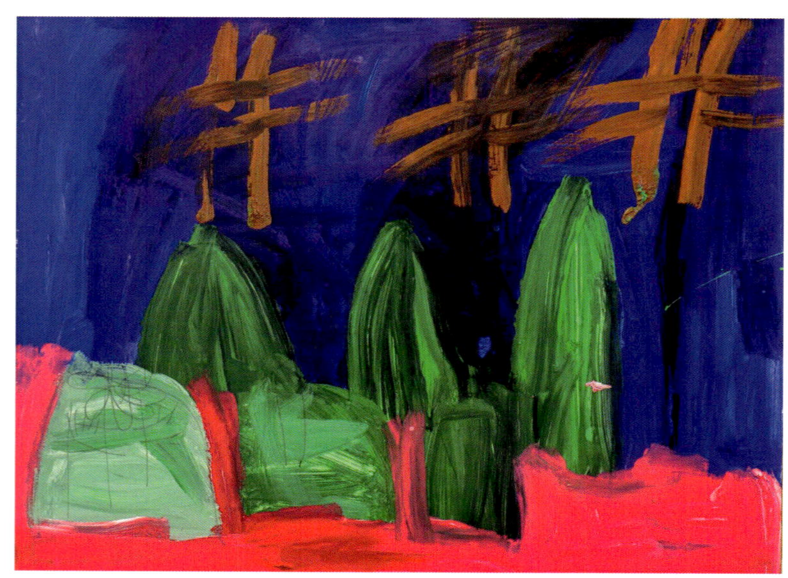

Hills and Trees
Painted in Portugal.
Acrylic on card, 2015.

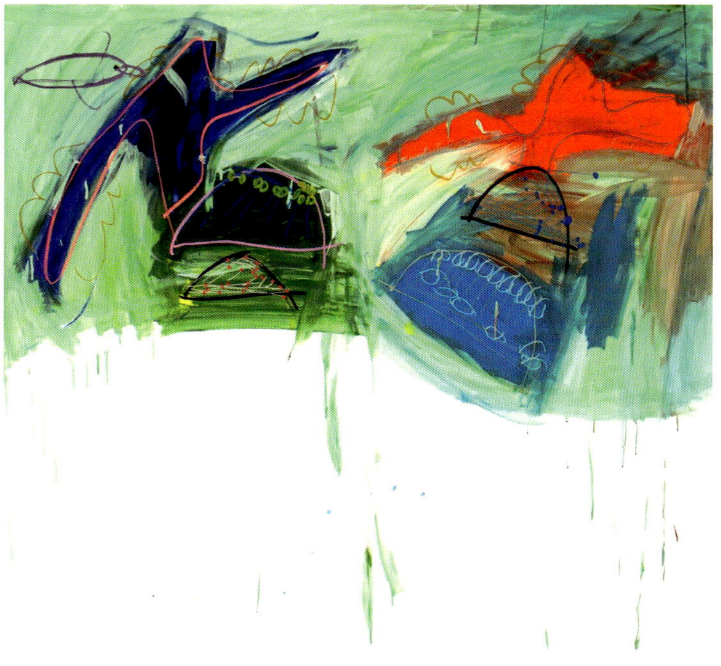

Hills and Trees
First addition of crops in the fields!
Acrylic on paper with added Posca pen,
2017, 151 x 111cm.

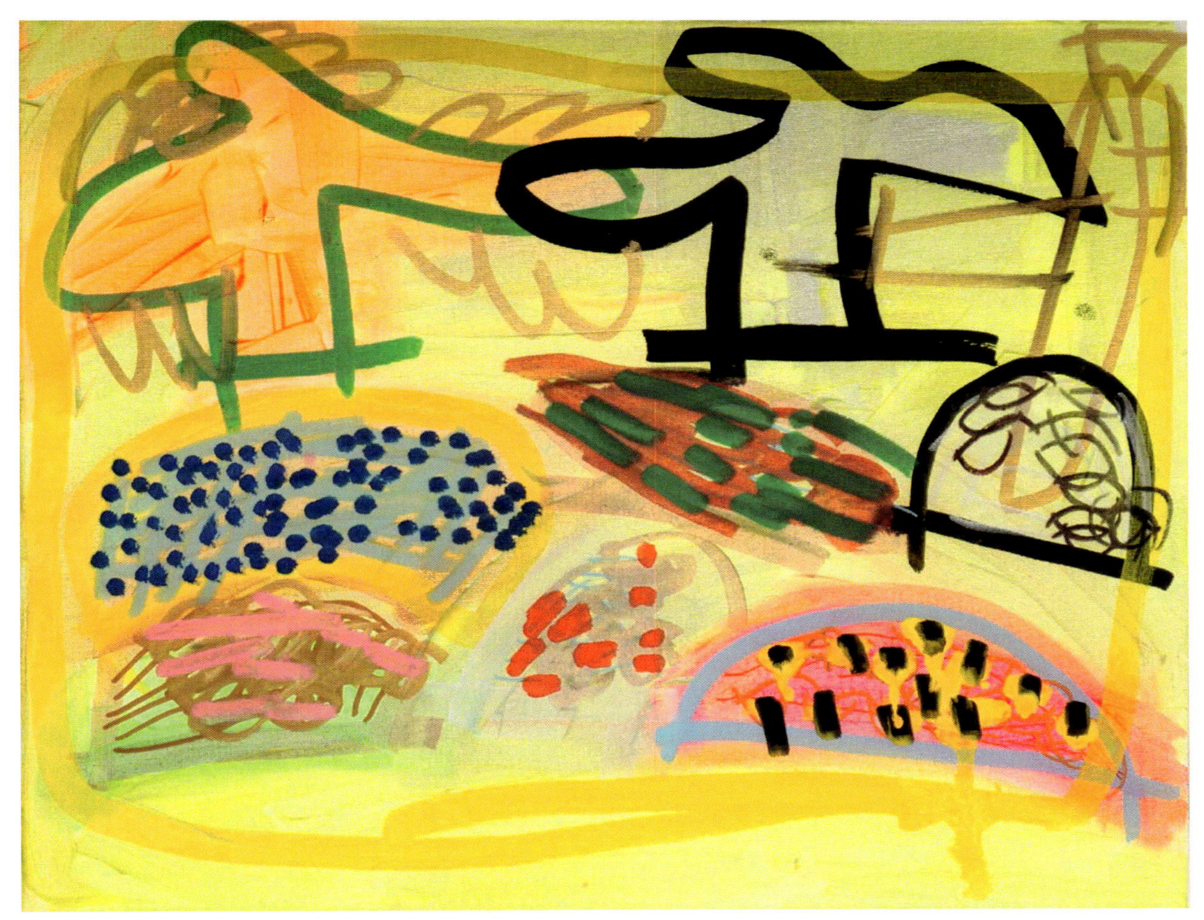

Early *Hills and Trees*. Acrylic on canvas, revisited with Posca pen, 2017.

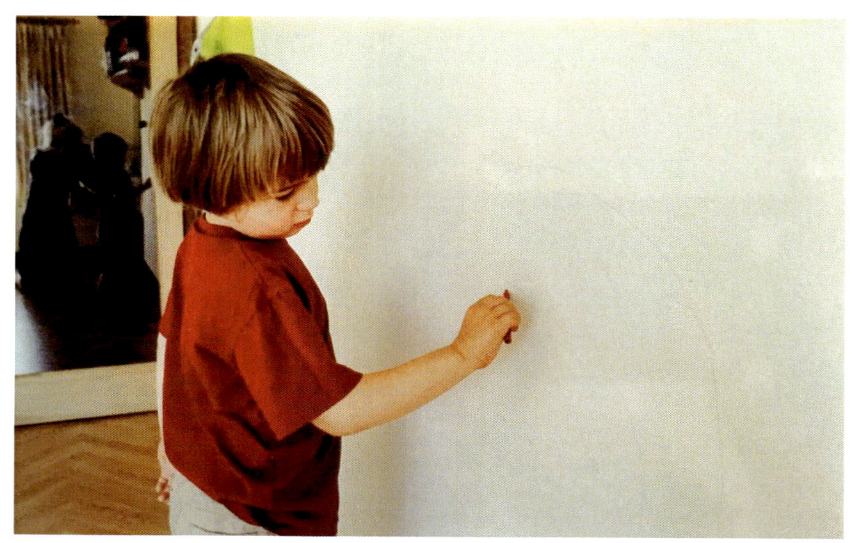

Rainbow
Johnny, aged 4, learning to make a mark.
With his mum in reflection.
Crayon on wall, 2002.

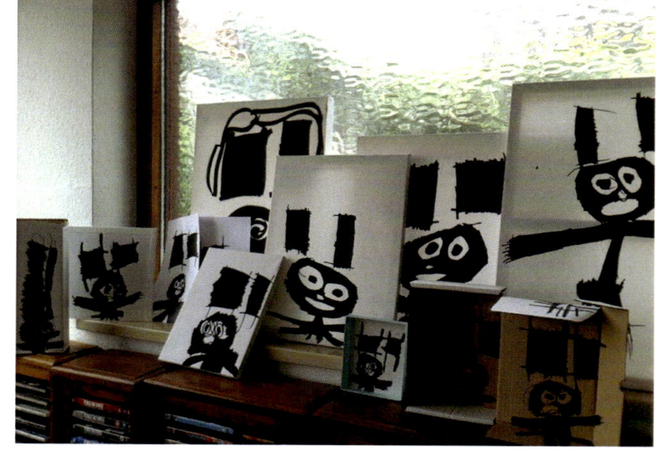

A collection of black and white *Kung Fu Pandas*
on separate canvases/cardboard boxes, c.2013.

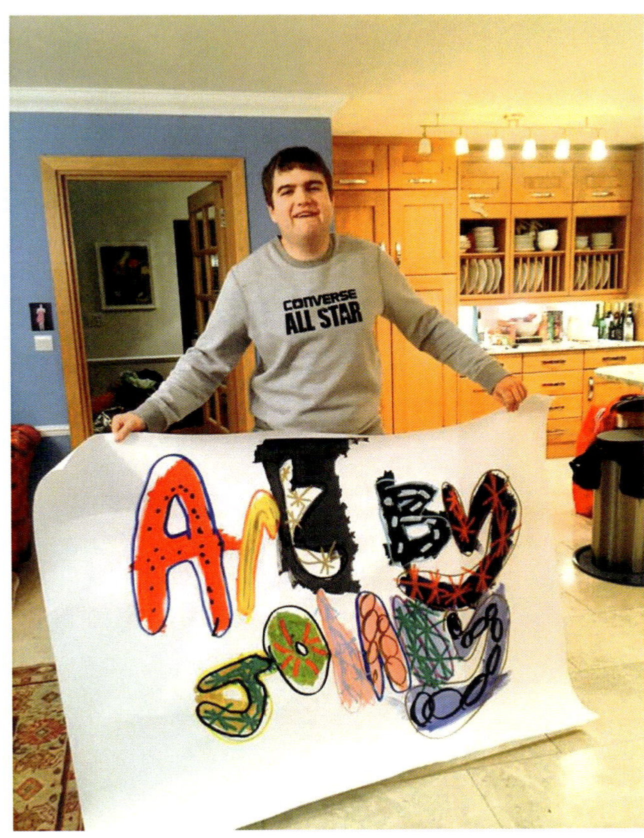

Johnny holding up his handwritten/painted
sign "Art By Johnny", 2017.

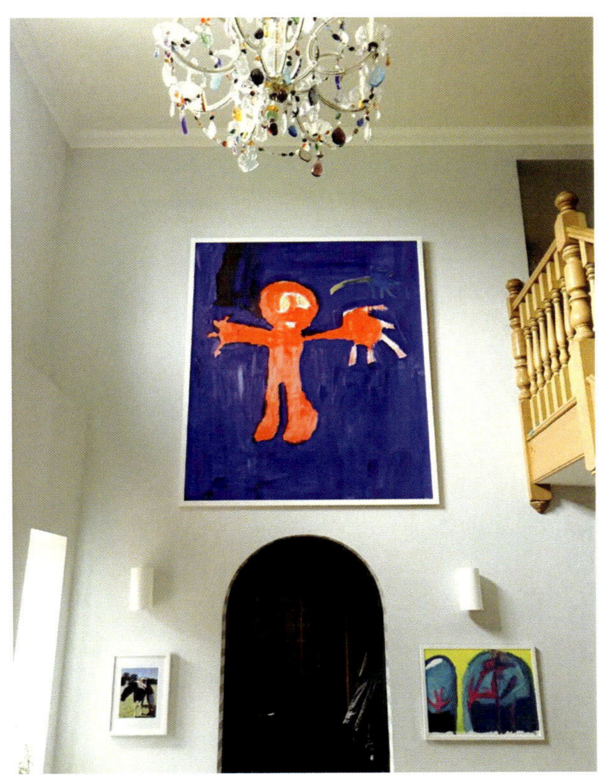

Giant Red Man framed above arch with smaller
View from Villa to one side.
Giant Red Man painted at Mymarc Saturday Art Club, 2016.
View from Villa painted c.2009, 145cm x 170cm.

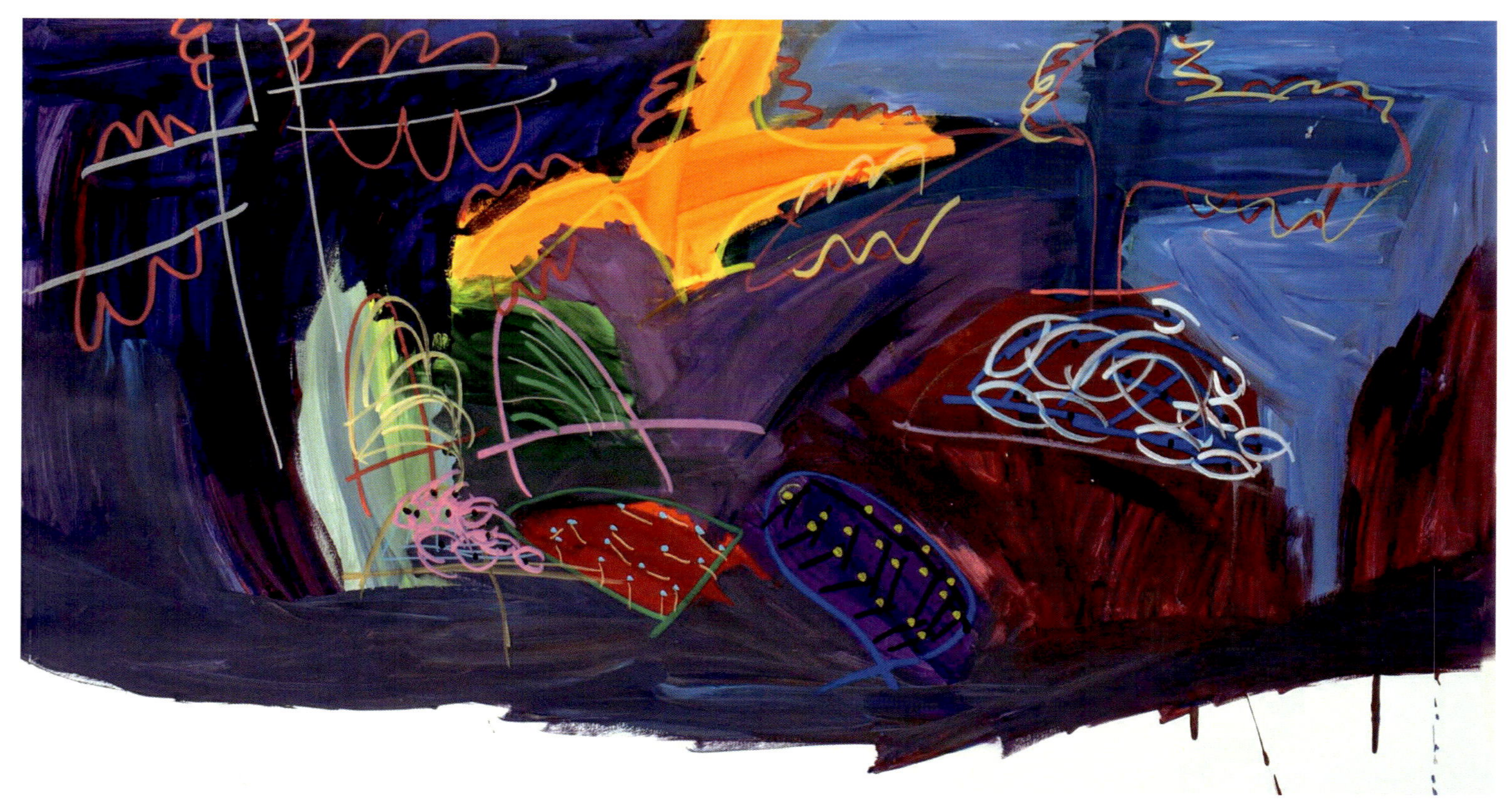

Hills and Trees
Saturday afternoon painting.
Acrylic on paper with added Posca pen, 2017, 151cm x 94cm.

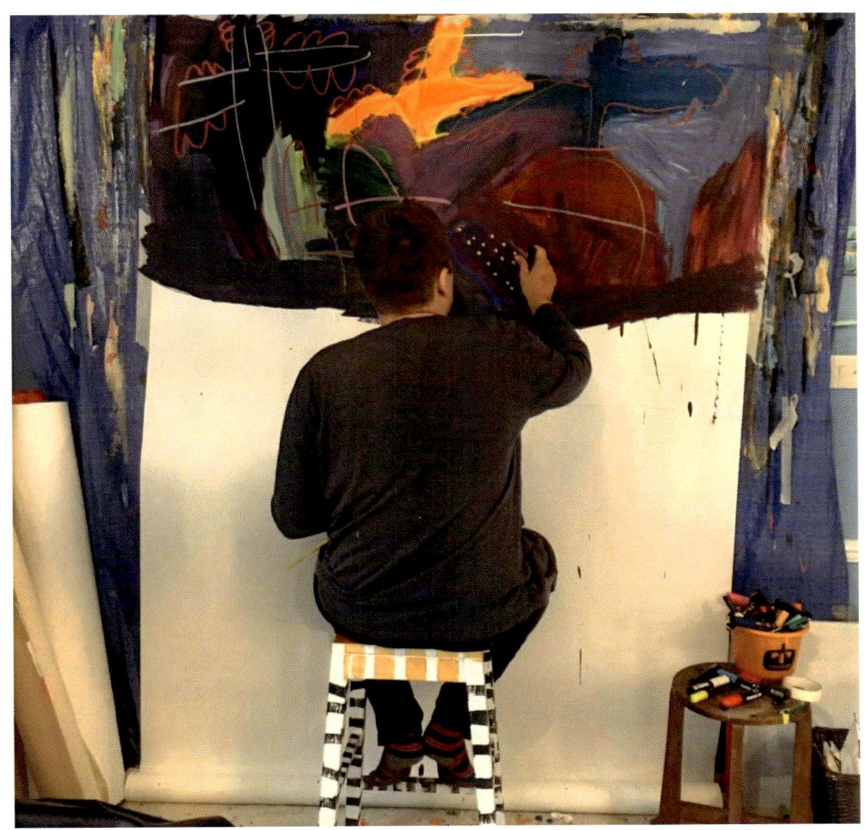

Johnny on painted stool applying
Posca pen to *Hills and Trees*.

Thanks to Jo Offer and the staff at Rocket Artists, Sue Winter and the staff at Mymarc, Martin Christie, Laura Keeble, Pete Ramskill, Denyce Aresti, Sara Harris, Thomas Rainsford, Paul Neads, Lisa Newman, Lindsay Hughes, Nick Taylor, Emily Hampshire, Jane Asher, Frank Cottrell Boyce, Jessica Hynes and everyone who has supported and encouraged Johnny's creativity over the years.

Photography by Martin Christie at colourfast.co.uk,
Angela Pell and Henry Normal.

Edited by Henry Normal.

Also by Henry Normal:

A Normal Family (Two Roads, 2018)
Raining Upwards (Flapjack Press, 2017)
Travelling Second Class Through Hope (Flapjack Press, 2017)
Staring Directly at the Eclipse (Five Leaves Publications, 2016)